The Magic Of The Pyramids
In Egypt

How they were formed

by

Reinhold Pachowsky
Real estate expert

4th edition 2024

Imprint
Bibliographic information of the German National Library:
The German National Library lists this publication in the German National Bibliography. Detailed bibliographic data is available on the Internet at http://dnb.dnb.de.

dlpVerlag.de
Nuremberg/Germany
Contact: office@dlpverlag.de

Cover photo:
Felix Peteranderl

The photos are printed in black and white in this book, but they where also available in color at:
www.pyramidenbau.immobilien-institut.de

page

Contents

Foreword

The famous pyramids

They are the landmark of Egypt and known worldwide: The pyramids near Giza and Cairo. They are around 4500 years old and have been studied many times. The question that remains unanswered is: HOW were they built?

I, a real estate expert and owner and director of the IMI Real Estate Institute, a recognized educational institute in Nuremberg, for around thirty years and author of many real estate books, have investigated this question in this book from the perspective of a property.

A property?

This may seem surprising at first, but if the pyramids were "built" from the bottom up according to previous theories, for example according to the "ramp theory", then they would be a building and therefore a property. The latter is nothing unusual.

The fundamental question is therefore: Can such a "mighty something" that is clearly visible in a special shape of the triangle on the earth have been built by the people of that time as a new building?

I have studied the pyramids in detail for years, read many scientific books and tried to understand all the usual building theories. I have visited the pyramids inside and out and traveled along the Nile from Cairo up to and including Lake Nasser to familiarize myself with the situation. However, you can only see today's greatly altered state and not how it was back then.

It is therefore important to put yourself in the shoes of that time around 4500 years ago. There is no doubt that the construction of the pyramids was a truly "huge task" that was solved ingeniously.

HOW this task was solved back then is the secret of these three pyramids in Giza near Cairo, but I presume to have found the solution.

However, another place in antiquity was decisive for the solution, namely Isfahan in today's Iran, then the Persian Empire. The earlier Persian culture was just as unique and the site is still somewhat more pristine and not yet as perfectly touristy as it is in Egypt. In any case, I found structural information there that allowed me to draw conclusions about the construction of the pyramids.

The construction of the pyramids should by no means be approached from today's technically advanced perspective, but in a practical way and - importantly - in the evolutionary context of the time.

After so many decades of stagnation on this issue, it is now time for a new approach that is above all true to life.

Please follow me now to Egypt 4500 years ago and to the question under which circumstances huge pyramids were created.

Reinhold Pachowsky

1. The fifth millennium BC

The three famous pyramids

I am standing on hot, sandy ground in front of the famous three pyramids in Egypt, waiting for Deniz Sahin, a local architect, to talk to me about the construction of the pyramids. Finally, a carriage pulls up and Sahin gets out with a broad smile.

"Sorry I'm late."
We shake hands and greet each other.

"As-salàmu àlaikum (good day)" I say, also smiling, "you're actually very punctual for an Egyptian". We laugh and after a short pause I say:

"I'd like to talk to you about the pyramids".

"Yes, I know that's what I'm here for".
He thinks for a moment and then says:

"To understand them the pyramids you have to go very far back into mankind's past". The roots of mankind lie in Central Africa and from there people moved out into the wide world. Egypt is relatively close by, so we can assume that the land around the Nile was already inhabited around five thousand years before Christ, long before the pyramids. And in this respect, it is not surprising that the first advanced civilization, the "Old Kingdom", was already established in Egypt around three thousand BC, when Europe was not yet recognizably populated and these pyramids were built.

"To build the pyramids, you have to go back a good four to five thousand years," says Sahin, "and since there are hardly any records, in many cases you have to make assumptions and use logic."
I see. So let's start by traveling back in time from today, for example:
↓ The computer age from after the year 2000
Computers were invented at this time and accelerated working life enormously.
↓ The industrialization
Electricity, steam drives and thus machines were invented.
↓ The Middle Ages

Knights and kings shaped the age.

↓ The Romans

Everyone knows the films with the marching soldiers in sandals with spears, bows and arrows, the chariots with two wheels pulled by horses and the chariot races, as well as the many kings of the time who fought for their power. The Romans already had a well-functioning administration and many things have been preserved to this day. Take Jesus, for example. He really existed, he had three older brothers (his sisters were not recorded), he was one of around three hundred preachers of his time - and Christianity was born.

↓ The Greeks

Famous Greeks invented important foundations of humanity. The Greek philosophers are still famous today.

↓ New kingdom of the Egyptians

The temples in Luxor are famous for this period and for the many famous tombs that have been found.

↓ Middle Kingdom of the Egyptians

The 11th to 14th dynasties move south to Sudan. Brick pyramids are built there.

↓ The Old Kingdom of the 1st to 3rd dynasties during which the three famous pyramids were built. This period is the focus of this book.

■ Predynastic period before the Egyptians

This rough outline is only intended to give a brief impression of the past because the period is often neglected in the literature on the pyramids and often even mixed up in an unprofessional manner.

"The period of the so-called "Old Kingdom" should not be confused with the later period," says Sahin, "and it is extremely important in relation to pyramid construction, especially with regard to possible tools and the craftsmanship of these Egyptians at that time.

The few people compared to today began to form villages shortly before the 1st Dynasty and thus societies and first rules of coexistence and thus "Egypt" (which was called differently at that time). The first king Narmer was probably the personality on the threshold of the 1st Dynasty who was able to lead his people to a unique upswing and initial prosperity. The population exploded and a new social mindset emerged. Ownership of land was created and a social hierarchy with farmers with and without their own land, craftsmen and specialists of various kinds, officials, scribes, priests and aristocrats such as the vizier called chati and, of course, the king as leader with divine claim.

"Their language has not been handed down, but language and writing are causally interdependent, meaning that one cannot exist without the other. So language is basically expressed in writing and the first hyroglyphs were created, which we still don't know how they were pronounced," I say.

"The environmental conditions of the time are also important," says Sahin. "The Nile in particular, with its regular floods, was the lifeline because the water brought fertile soil that offered good conditions for productive agriculture. We'll certainly come back to that."

"Absolutely," I say, "in this context, I'm particularly interested in the emergence of craftsmen as a professional group with further subgroups of specialists, for example the potters, the clothes makers and the builders who built mastabas, i.e. tombs, and invented the Nile brick as a building material for buildings of all kinds."
And I say to Sahin:

"So if you were building buildings, you had to know beforehand how to build from the bottom of the earth upwards in principle. Because if the pyramids were built from the bottom up, then the rules of construction also applied to them."

"The basic rules that apply to all types of buildings all over the world are
a. You need a plot of land and a builder to finance the building.
b. Then the imaginary building is measured and classified on this plot.

c. Next, a foundation is excavated on the measured plot and the excavated material is moved to the side or driven away.

d. Now the foundation, which today is usually made of concrete, must be made. Back then it was mostly made of tamped clay.

e. The walls are erected on the foundation and joined together for structural reasons.

f. Then comes a roof, which here in Egypt is usually a simple flat roof because it hardly ever rains.

"So there are six steps," I confirm.

"Those were just the visible points on the outside. Of course, there's also the interior work, so building in general is a very complex process."

"What concerns me is: how did a pharaoh comparable to a king actually come up with the idea of a pyramid back then?"

"Good question," says Sahin with a smile, "but I don't know. As an architect, I can only say that this triangular shape, which rises steeply from each side and yet is a square that is exactly at an angle, is revolutionary in itself compared to the very simple mud houses of the people."

"And the even more important question for me - and probably for all real estate experts - is the location: why do the three pyramids stand in a desert far outside the center and thus in an inhospitable and remote area even then?

The later and much later rulers of the Greeks and Romans always wanted to be buried "close to their people" and thus "in the middle of the action", which is probably the natural need of a ruler. The center at the time of Cheops was Memphis, a six-hour walk through the desert."

2. The location

The places of that time: Giza Sakkara Memphis

Today, the pyramids are located in Giza near Cairo. Around 4500 years ago, Giza and Cairo did not exist. The capital of the "Old Kingdom" at that time (officially 2640 - 2465 BC) was Memphis (see above) and therefore 28 km away from the pyramids. Memphis must have been a beautiful green city under palm trees and was of great importance as the "city of the ruler" with temples, administrative buildings, etc. It was the seat of the pharaohs of the time. The buildings were obviously not made of stone because none of them are still there today, only the colossal statue of Rames II lying on his back, which has nothing to do with the "Old Kingdom".

3. The Pharaonic Dynasty

The pyramids were built in the "Old Kingdom" of the 3rd to 6th dynasties. Little information has survived from the 1st and 2nd dynasties. In any case, this "Old Kingdom" was an up-and-coming era in which mastabas (private tombs), rock tombs, royal statues, the first handicrafts (jewelry, vases, etc.), private portraits and reliefs and pyramids were created for the first time.

* The dynasties of this period

The 3rd Dynasty began with the reign of King Djoser (the term "pharaoh" was probably only introduced later in the Middle Kingdom). He had the first pyramids built (to follow under point 4). He is regarded as the most important ruler of this 3rd dynasty. His capital was

Sakkara, where he had the first step pyramid built from stone instead of mud brick.

"This use of stones in architecture instead of the previous Nile clay bricks was a new stage of development in the art of building," says Sahin with conviction.

"We should still talk about the details," I say.

During this period of the "Old Kingdom", there were the following kings of the same dynasty after Djoser:
* Snofru from about 2570 to 2545 BC
* Cheops from about 2545 to 2520 BC
* son Djedefe (pyramid begun in Abu Roash)
* Half-brother Chephren from about 2510 to around 2485 BC
* Son Mykerinos until about 2471 BC.

* King Cheops and his family
Cheops was the king who had the largest of the three pyramids built. There is only a small statue of him, only a few centimeters tall, on display in the Egyptian Museum.

Cheops had fourteen children with three to four wives and lived to be about sixty years old. No palace or tomb has been found.

Characteristics of King CHEOPS	
Other names	Chufu Jufu Khufu Suphis
Epoch:	Old Empire
Dynasty:	2. King of the 4. Dynasty
Reign:	ca. 2579 - 2556 v.Chr. approx. 23 years ca. 2620 - 2580 v.Chr. approx. 40 years
Father:	Snofru *)
Mother:	Hetepheres
Siblings:	Chephren (Halfbrother) Anchchaf (Halfbrother *) Henutsen (Halfsister) (after A. Siliotti) Hetepheres (Halfbrother *) Nefermaat (Halfbrother *) Nefretkau (Halfsister *) Rehotep (Halbbruder *)
Wives:	Henutsen (nach A. Siliotti) Hetephernebti (after W. Helck) Königin Meritites *
Children:	Anchchaf (after R. Stadelmann) Bafra * Chafchufui (after R. Stadelmann) Chamerernebti * Chafmin * Chephren *) Djedefhor *) Djedefmin *) Djedefra *) Duenhor *) Hetepheres II. *) Kawab *) Meresanch II. *)

Source: www.eglyphica.de   *) nach Schneider

"The fact that there were kings for the first time in the Old Kingdom", I say to Sahin, "leads to the conclusion that the small villages mentioned at the beginning must have grown into large village communities and understood themselves as "one people"".

"Yes," he says, "there must have been a population explosion due to the relatively favorable living conditions on the Nile and people learned from each other - today it's called "leaning by doing" - invented new, simple tools and used them. For their own housing, they invented the aforementioned Nile brick, a material made of mud and plants pressed into a template and dried, which was very suitable for building."

And when there are many people, a leader is needed, a king who stands above the people even more:

Every pharaoh-king must have regarded himself as a god in terms of belief in gods and also in all worldly matters. His word was law. And his death led to a change of power which, unlike in later times, was not extreme in this period because the successors were descended in a direct line from the royal house of the previous dynasty. This does not rule out internal struggles for power.

So there was a king as absolute ruler, a dictator who told his people what to do and what not to do. This is still the case today in many countries around the world. The pyramids were a clear external symbol of this power.

4. The pyramids

"The pyramids probably had the purpose of a tomb" says architect Sahin "but they could also have been understood as a "sacred religious site", for example as the "dwelling place for eternity" or also mystically as the visible transition from man to the sun to the sky to the gods".

Three of the four pharaoh kings did indeed erect a monument for eternity with these pyramids:
- Cheops pyramid (= Great Pyramid)
- Pyramid of Chephren (= middle pyramid)
- Mykerinos pyramid (= small pyramid)

This book is primarily concerned with these three pyramids, but with the Great Pyramid of Cheops and specifically with the question of its construction.
First, however, they will be presented in more detail:

The Cheops pyramid

It is the oldest and largest or highest pyramid

at Giza and is therefore rightly referred to as the "Great Pyramid".

"This designation is certainly correct," says architect Sahin, "because it consists of an estimated or calculated three million stone blocks, each weighing 25 tons or more. It was clad with limestone slabs and is

- a height of 146,6 m
  (today 138,75m because the top is
   missing)
  in comparison: almost as high as a
  skyscraper with 50 storeys (!)

- a side length of 238,7 m
  in comparison: like 40 standard
  terraced houses (!)

- an angle of inclination of 51°50'
  much steeper than a pitched roof and
  not accessible

- a floor area of 53,000 square meters
  i.e. approx. 13 football pitches

- and a volume of 2,583,283 m³.

"This size is unique!" he cheers "No one has ever built anything on this scale again! It is precisely aligned with the four points of the compass," says the architect proudly, "and it stands at an exact geometric angle. The construction time is estimated at around 20 - 25 years (with an almost inhuman daily output). Completion of the building was set for around 2580 BC."

The pyramid of Cheops in 2015

To make it clear once again:
We are talking about a colossus that is 40 terraced houses (side by side) wide and 50 stories high at the top! And so steep that it is not accessible in the normal way.

The Chephren pyramid

Djedefe, the son of Cheops wanted to outdo his father - as many sons often do - by building an even higher pyramid - and failed miserably. Cheops' half-brother Chephren was next in line. Why he and not his son is not known.

The pyramid of Chephren (Khafre) in 2015

"The pyramid of Khafre is considered the second highest of the three pyramids of Giza. Nevertheless, on closer inspection it appears higher than the pyramid of Khufu, but this is due to its steeper angle of inclination of 53°10' and the slightly higher ground. It is only relatively slightly smaller because it has a

- height of 136,4 m
  which corresponds to about 44 floors of a
  skyscraper

- a side length of 215,25 m
  which corresponds to about 35 terraced
  houses

- an angle of inclination of 53°10'
It is therefore also very steep and cannot be
walked on

- its volume is 2,211,096 m³."

According to its name, it was probably built as
a tomb for Pharaoh-King Khafre. As far as is
known, he was also buried here at the time.
According to more recent findings, he
probably also had the giant sphinx built in
front of the pyramids (see below).

The Mykerinos pyramid

"It is the smallest of the three pyramids
of Giza, but overall it is one of the top 10
highest Egyptian pyramids and was probably
also built as a tomb for the Pharaoh-King
Mykerinos (= son of Pharaoh Chephren) who
reigned in the 4th dynasty from around 2532
to 2503 BC.
It has a
- height of 62 m (originally 65 m), which is
  "only" about 21 storeys
- a side length of 1022 m by 1046 so
  like about 17 terraced houses

and

- an angle of inclination of 51°50', which means that it is visually just as steep as the other two".

The Mykerinos pyramid in 2015

There is no documentation as to why it is smaller and therefore more modest, only conjecture, as he was the last king of this dynasty and there were much worse times to come. Times of drought, as we know today.

Inside, by the way, all three pyramids are different in detail.

The Sphinx

We continue to the nearby Sphinx.
In front of the three pyramids - as seen from the main entrance - there is a large sphinx about whose meaning and purpose there is no documentation. We can therefore only make assumptions and one obvious one is that it was created as a "protective god".

However, there are also studies according to which the sphinx is much older and was created before the pyramids.

The Sphinx arranged before the pyramids

"According to more recent findings," says Sahin, "King Khafre had it built. It seems clear that it was carved out of a boulder. Recently, underground passages and rooms have been found. However, these have not yet been explored, or only to a limited extent. The Sphinx could therefore have been created from a completely different situation".

Why were the pyramids built?

"What interests me much more," I mean, "is the answer to the question: Why were pyramids built and how did the Pharons - let's stick with this name - come up with the idea of designing the pyramids in a triangle?"

(The Pythagorean theorem known to us and thus the shape of the triangle was only mathematically invented much later, around 570 BC. Or was it invented much earlier by the Egyptians?)

"The starting point," Sahin begins, "is probably that there must have been a pronounced mortuary culture even before the 1st Dynasty. The pyramids played a special role in this. In any case, death was not understood as something final but as the "transition into darkness" or as a transition to the sun and the sky.

Just as the sun reappears in the morning, the deceased also return at some point and they should be provided with burial objects for this long journey. This was probably the principle of the belief, which is still the case today but does not explain the pyramids. What is striking is the shape pointing upwards towards the sky, similar to an index finger. And when a person raises their index finger, it is usually for something that is very important to them. This is how they could have been understood: As a widely visible landmark for something very important for a "new world".

Death is still omnipresent in Africa today because people of all ages die of blood poisoning, drugs, accidents, murder and disease every day, at least more than anywhere else. Death is part of life - that was and still is the "primal belief" of the people there. This understanding is important when dealing with the pyramids.

It seems that the Egyptians were a spiritually highly developed people. The people of that time were just as intelligent as we are today because every newborn child always starts at "0", just like today: there was not so much information because there was no writing to pass it on to their descendants.

They had not yet invented the wheel, but they already had the beginnings of writing: hyroglyphs. However, nothing written has been found of the construction of the pyramids. Only the temples in Luxor, 1000 to 2000 years later, were densely described.

With regard to the pyramids and the reason why they were built, one must therefore concentrate on a landmark, a "landmark for something very important".
As if he could read minds, Sahin begins:

"Science assumes that the sun was the most important phenomenon at the time and therefore "God": it rises in the morning and returns to darkness in the evening. This process was certainly incomprehensible and uncanny at the time. Would the sun really come back the next day? After all, it was (and is) the most important thing for all life on earth.
People used gods to explain inexplicable phenomena such as the sun, death, the Nile, the weather and so on. And over time, more than five hundred gods were created for this purpose.
People need leadership and clear rules from two people upwards. That was the position of the pharaoh, the "king".

From his point of view, the motive was clear: I am the "divine" or "godlike" and as such the protector of the people. That is why I need a tomb that radiates "my greatness" for eternity. The realization was successful. Apparently he was able to persuade or force the people to work for him on the pyramid all day long for days and months in enormous heat. Presumably for little pay. And there will certainly have been serious injuries and deaths at this major construction site. Under these harsh conditions, which were (and are) in addition to the already difficult living conditions, people generally only work under two conditions: Power and violence or religion and faith.

So at least one religion was needed and this consisted of belief in gods. Above all, the sun was worshipped because all life depended on it and the pharaoh-king was the symbol of the sun.

As the protector of the people, it was believed that he could only exercise this protective function after his death if the people built a suitable "staircase" for him to ascend to the sun in time for the realm of the dead. And so that no one else could presume to do this and also climb up, it was made so steep that it was impassable.

The pyramid may therefore have been the symbol and landmark of an "important stairway to heaven". Through the building, the people received mystical protection from the king, even after his death. This protection was the people's reward for their work.

5. First pyramids

The Giza pyramids were not the first. A good 100 years before the Giza pyramids, King Djoser had the first so-called "step pyramid" built on the other side of the desert, which was "only" around 60 meters high. It is located in what was then the center of Saqqara (~ Sakkara).
The masonry is clearly visible. The tomb was originally lined with limestone. Limestone is a white stone, so the pyramid must have shone beautifully in the sunshine.

The step pyramid Source 1)

This step pyramid is the first building of this time in which stones were used instead of mud bricks, making it the first stone building! The use of stone is attributed to a man who was apparently also the construction manager but primarily a scholar. His name: Imhotep.

Master builder Imhotep

He was a well-educated physician, writer and author of a wisdom doctrine. The use of stone in architecture can be traced back to him. The way he used it reveals a completely new building concept, namely the replacement of Nile mudstones in favor of stone. Source 1)

Imhotep scholar doctor construction manager and "inventor" of the construction method using stones instead of Nilemudbricks Source 3)

Step pyramid and surrounding desert 2015
Remains of a stone wall surrounding the pyramid

The Bent Pyramid in Dashur

Pharaoh's successor Snofru had three pyramids built for himself in Dahshur around 2550 BC. These were the Red Black Pyramid and the Bent Pyramid.

The Bent Pyramid 2015

The latter was so named because - as can be seen - it has a kink in it and looks a little misshapen. You can still clearly see that a smooth layer was applied to the stones, presumably to make them shine in the sunlight.

And even centuries earlier there were smaller pyramids made of mudstones in what is now Sudan. They were estimated to be around 6 to 8 meters high. However, only a few of the originals still exist because the mud bricks dry out and disintegrate after a while. However, there are still said to be around 200 similar pyramids in Sudan. And there were also smaller pyramids made of Nile mud in Egypt which were later replaced by stone structures.

A photo of the first pyramids Source 2)

The desert and the stone structure

Seen from the Nile, all three pyramids in Giza stand high up on a limestone plateau. This is not a plain but rather a large "wild sandstone desert" with valleys and hills that stretches from the Nile delta on the left and right side of the Nile more than 1000 km south to Asuan and into Sudan.

From the Nile, which today is relatively far away from the pyramids, there is a steady and sometimes steep ascent to the pharaonic site.

There are several similar deserts on earth and they are almost always criss-crossed by faults, gorges and mesas.

A striking feature of the Pharaonic site is that the desert floor consists not only of sand but also of a coarse, brittle calcareous sandstone.

Sand-lime brick consisting of sand and lime

6. The Nile and the "Old Kingdom"

The Nile is (with the Amazon) the longest river in the world and today is about 1 - 2 kilometers wide at the pyramids. At that time, the Nile determined the rhythm of life and the year.

Nile and desert 2015

In August, a flood of water arrived in Egypt from the mountains (Sudan Ethiopia) and flooded the landscape to the left and right of the Nile all the way to the delta in the Mediterranean. This rain was - and still is - caused by the monsoon and thus by the heavy rainfall in the Ethiopian highlands with mountains more than 4000 meters high, in the period from May to August. The moving tidal wave reached the Nile and at the pyramids its highest level of an average of two meters above the normal level from the end of September to the beginning of October at the same time every year. Only the flood itself varied and low levels meant drought crop failure famine.

Photo Nile flood villages around 1830 Source 29)

Unlike people today, who usually panic when flooding occurs, people back then probably retreated to their mud-built shelters in good time and waited for the flood. This was desirable because the sediments (deposits) carried with them formed the Nile mud and thus the basis for the agricultural land. The mud settled and thus moistened the soil. Sowing then took place and it was three to four months before the harvest. Then the soil was dry again and no farming was possible. At that time, however, people had already invented an irrigation system with canals to improve the area and cultivation time.

Near Aswan on the island of Elephantine, there was and still is a "Nilometer" on which the level of the Nile can be read. It has been handed down that it was later used in the New Kingdom to calculate the flooded area and thus to determine the taxes payable to the pharaoh.

The Egyptians in the "Old Kingdom", who were of course not yet aware of the climatic connections between the flooding of the Nile, gave this process a mythological meaning. The deity Apophis was responsible because the flood came regularly. It was heralded by a green colouring of the Nile water (caused by algae) and the Egyptians were able to recognize the actual flood wave that began in mid-July by the reddish discoloration of the river water for which Apophis was responsible. After reaching the highest water level between the end of August and the beginning of September, the black Nile mud sank to the bottom of the fields. Egypt is therefore called "black land" because of the sediment deposits. Periods of low tides meant less flooded and therefore less fertile land, resulting in crop failures and famine. Floods that were too high, in turn, caused damage to buildings (as is basically still the case today).

The cultivation and breeding of plants for subsistence was a major evolutionary step, as these were still the "original people" who, according to tradition, mainly roamed the land as nomads in southern Africa and mainly kept animals, as is still the case in many African countries today.

Not so with the Egyptians of that time. They walked upright, bare-chested, wore a loincloth and lived mainly from the produce of agriculture. They were already farmers. Animals, especially donkeys, cows and camels, were mainly kept as livestock.

Farming had to be carried out in the blazing sun and heat until October, when it was around 30 - 40 degrees in the shade. When the tide receded, the plants were planted and harvested after about three months to provide food for the people and animals for the rest of the year. This also applied to the pharaoh, the officials and the priests. The latter arose due to the rapidly growing population.
I consider it unlikely that work was also carried out on the pyramids during this time, i.e. 365 days a year and even on the hottest days of the year. This also does not correspond to the mentality (follows).

Men building Source 1)

Only after the harvest season did people possibly have time to deal with other things, such as the construction of houses and utility buildings from Nile mud bricks. Unlike other authors, I therefore assume that the people did not work on the tombs and pyramids all year round but only outside the Nile flood and harvest time, i.e. for a maximum of nine months from November to July. Vital agriculture certainly had priority. Because outside the Nile Valley there was only desert and therefore nothing to earn a living.

Over time, however, professional craftsmen may have emerged for stone carving and artistic work (vases, jewelry, figurines).

Jug around 2570 BC Source 1)

The "state of the art" thus continued to expand during this period of the Old Kingdom, namely from agriculture to craftsmen, depending on talent and aptitude. Today we would say that craftsmanship and thus new professions emerged at that time, probably also trade, as the import of cedar wood has been recorded. In any case, these are further evolutionary steps!

The people of ancient Egypt practiced agriculture with simple tools, bred domestic animals and thus had a very close relationship not only with nature but also with the weather, sun, moon and stars, as is known from primitive peoples.

This is understandable because when they looked up into the sky without glasses or binoculars, the events up there could only tell them that there must be gods.

Life on the Nile 4500 years ago

In order to understand the time of the pyramids, you have to go back to the ancient Egypt of the "Old Kingdom". So let's not beam ourselves into the future, but into the past! So if you go back to 4500 years ago, the situation back then could have been similar to what it still is today in Central Africa. For example, I myself spent several months in Gambia Namibia Tanzania Kenya Zanzibar and tour guide Christina Gottschall sums up the mentality in her travel book "Sansibar":

"When I was in West Africa I became calm.
When I arrived in East Africa I realized
that I was not yet calm enough".
Source 7)

This means that life in East Africa - compared to the rest of the world - is incredibly slow, even slower than in slow West Africa, i.e. almost in slow motion from the perspective of Western Europeans. People are in no hurry. If something needs to be done, they respond with a word that means: it can be done tomorrow, next week, next year or never. In my opinion, this serenity comes from the weather. Every day the sun shines in the blue sky every day is like the next day so why this (European-Western) hurry?

Nubian village today Source 2)
Now that there is no more flooding of the Nile, we can build right up to the banks.

The reason: there is no winter. From the fall onwards, nothing grows in Europe and you have to take precautions for the cold winter, i.e. work faster. But not in Africa. The relatively uniform hot weather has become ingrained in the genes and hormones over the millennia, which can be seen externally in the (varying degrees of) brown skin and in the serenity. Sitting together drinking tea and discussing all topics in detail and calmly is still a custom today.

However, building the pyramids at high speed over 365 days, as some Western scientists believe in order to justify the calculated construction time of the pyramids, is by no means part of the mentality.

In today's Egypt in the urban areas of Cairo, Giza or Memphis, the donkey cart (two wheels on two planks and a donkey in front) is still a common means of transportation. Progress is still correspondingly slow today.

Life 4500 years ago was at least just as slow and simple and largely "speed-free". Time played no role, only the daily rhythm of the sun alternating with the night. It is wrong to want to apply Western tempo standards here. As if Sahin had guessed my thoughts, he suddenly says:

"For the correct assessment of Egyptian architecture it is necessary to see it in the context of its historical development that is, the religious geographical and social contexts of the time apply."
It should not be overlooked that the simple tools of the time did not allow for a fast pace.
The tools give an impression of the working methods of the time.

Typical tools and working methods

The shovel, axe and spade were typical implements and predominant tools. These tools were still depicted on the temple columns in Luxor 1000 years later. However, it can be assumed that they were necessary for farmers even earlier in the "Old Kingdom". The material for these tools is wood, namely imported cedar and bamboo, which are relatively hard when dried and do not break easily.

Middle row: Working tools

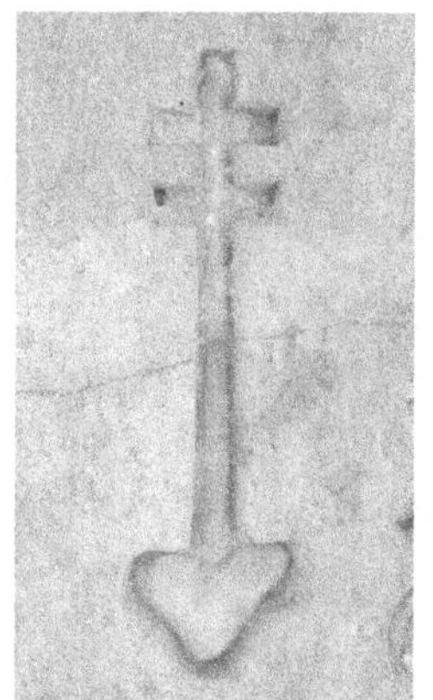

Spade and axe

It is not clear from these illustrations what these tools were actually made of. It is likely to have been wood. Copper and bronze were probably also known, but not iron. And the use of animals for transportation was a major advance.

Workers with animals Source 1)

Men at work with papyrus Source 1)

Pharaoh with tools Source 1)

Transportation at this time

The general transportation system of this period is important for pyramid building and stone transportation. People used animals such as donkeys, cows and camels for transportation.

Working with a donkey Source 1)

As a rule, however, everything was done by hand. As there was no wheel, wooden rails (runners) are easy to imagine (see picture). It was also possible to make ropes from palm leaves, hemp grass, papyrus and even leather for clothing. Hemp grass and reeds were twisted into rope. Ropes made from hemp grass are very strong.

Animal transportation around 2310 BC Source 1)

According to science, it is certain that leverage and the inclined plane were already being used to transport goods of all kinds.

In the Nile there were fish, the hippopotamus and crocodiles. That is why there was also hunting with a boat made of bamboo. These animals were probably also traded in exchange for other goods.

Hippo hunt with spear in a papyrus thicket
naked in a papyrus boat around 2340 BC Source 1)
In addition to crocodiles, there were also the Nile goose, the Nile grass rat and the Nile monitor lizard

The specialists

In addition to the craftsmen mentioned above, there may also have been a small circle of specialists who professionally worked stones or clay into vases, made beautiful jewelry and clothing and already lived from barter or trade. This would be the third evolutionary step in this dynasty.

The men wore a loincloth and were otherwise naked. Women of the upper class (only these are depicted) usually wore a long dress and often also jewelry and headdresses.

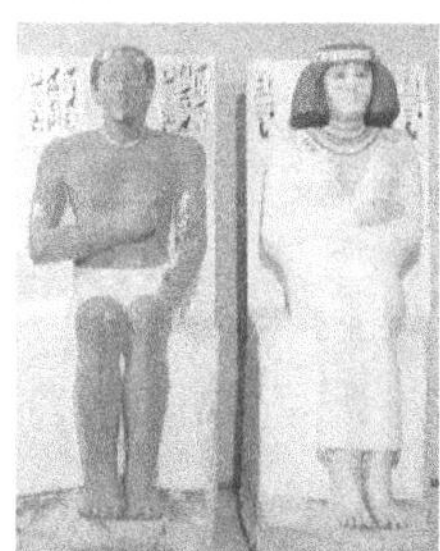
Source Egyptian Museum
Couple from the upper class known by name

Typical construction method with mud bricks

"The typical construction method in Egypt at this time 4500 years ago was the Nile mud brick," says the architect. "It was used for the construction of all buildings."
It was made as follows:
- Mix moist clay from the Nile with straw
- Pour into an elongated wooden mold
- leave to dry in the sun and
- and stack the walls stone by stone.

It soon became clear to them that a simple wall would simply fall over at a height of about one meter - depending on the ground - and that the only way to build higher was with a double-walled wall (two walls supporting each other) up to about two meters and connecting it with a roof construction so that it would remain standing (today called "statics"). The roof of these simple, often round houses was made of wood and palm and papyrus leaves turned into thatch. Walls were also built for boundaries. Example:

Remains of adobe buildings Source 1)

The double wall made of mud bricks is clearly visible. Clay building was undoubtedly an important achievement for the formation of villages and thus of great social importance for the village community. A clay house also creates a pleasant and healthy indoor climate for summer and winter because the clay has a temperature-balancing effect. In summer, when it is very hot outside, rooms in a clay house are pleasantly cool, and in the colder months it also has a regulating effect and protects against excessively dry indoor air.

Example: Today's Nubian village near Aswan

The Nubian people live in the south of Egypt. A long time ago, they moved from what is now Sudan to the north. Their houses are still simple buildings built with stones from the desert and supplemented with bricks from the Nile clay. The roof is made of thatch and wood. This is still the predominant construction method there today, which is often shown (and is also impressively simple).

Nubian village near Aswan 2015

Small people and a vegetarian diet

People back then were much smaller and slimmer than they are today. We know from the tombs of the Romans (more than 2000 years later) that adults were on average (only) between 090 and 120 m tall. Today, this is roughly equivalent to a ten-year-old child. A man of 140 m was already a "giant".
In ancient Egypt - another two thousand years ago - people were probably only up to about one meter tall on average, as can be seen from the size of the excavated sarcophagi. A modern human would not fit in there.

Short lifespan

Not only were people significantly smaller (today they are getting bigger and bigger), but life expectancy was only thirty years on average, which means that if you subtract a childhood of 10 years and an old age of 5 years, the productive period was only 15 years! This is probably why child labor was taken for granted.
At least two generations - of working age - must have worked on the pyramids.

They could not have been as well fed as today's Egyptians because the quantity and variety of food was not given. Today's

Egyptians also eat a largely vegetarian diet because meat and fish are expensive.

Small people of the upper class Source 1)

* Fish and meat no fire no rain

In addition to vegetarian food, only fish and hippopotamus meat were probably eaten in everyday life.

Everything was probably eaten raw because there is no evidence that people (already) knew about and used fire.

For example, in the 1000 year later temple in Luxor many everyday scenes are depicted but there is not a single sign of fire or rain. However, both are important natural phenomena that would certainly have been depicted.

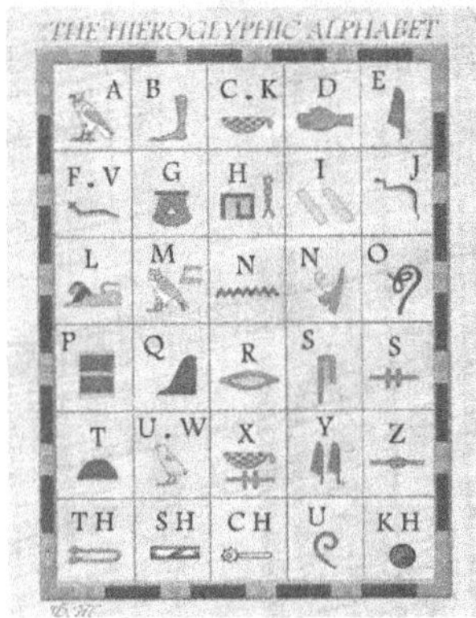

A much later hieroglyphic alphabet (N zigzag for Nile?) was still in its infancy at the time the pyramids were built, but how might these hieroglyphs have been pronounced back then?

There is no sign for water or fire in the hieroglyphs because when there was no rain there was no thunderstorm and no lightning. So how would people back then have known about fire? It therefore stands to reason that nothing could be cooked in the Old Kingdom due to a lack of fire. Apart from reeds and

papyrus, there were only bushes, no or hardly any trees, so there was no usable wood.
Perhaps there was occasional brief rain in the form of showers, but not a significant amount.

(A flight in a balloon shows that even today the houses have no roofs - in the western sense).

Evolutionary steps

In this period of the 3rd Dynasty of the Old Kingdom from 2528 BC to 2471 BC, i.e. around 150 years, i.e. 5 generations from Pharaoh Cheops to Pharaoh Mykerinos, in which the pyramids were built, the following evolutionary steps of humans have been handed down:
- Walking upright (probably even before that)
- Settling down through agriculture
- Production of mud bricks for the
  construction of houses and buildings
- The hieroglyphic script is created
- Establishment of a craftsmanship (stone
  metze) with creative variations (vase jewelry)
- Transition of the construction method from
  mud bricks to stone buildings. However,
  columns did not yet exist
- Production and wearing of clothing
- Production and use of simple tools
  tools (spade, axe)
- transportation of goods and trade.

And then suddenly and abruptly during this period there is supposed to have been a huge evolutionary "leap in technology" to build the pyramids?

Without any legacy, because in the following millennia of the Middle and New Kingdoms, no corresponding technology has been handed down.

7. The initial structural situation: The three-part structure of the pyramids

Many authors have already dealt with the structural side of the pyramids, but now I have the unique opportunity to interview an expert architect. I begin our conversation with:

"Let's talk about the main topic, the pyramids."

"It's taken a long time, but prior knowledge of the period is extremely important. The structure of the pyramids is now clear. They consist of a core masonry, which is the

a. inner core of the pyramid,

b. a facing masonry and

c. a façade, i.e. stones that were placed on the outside of the masonry."

Sahin shows me the following picture:

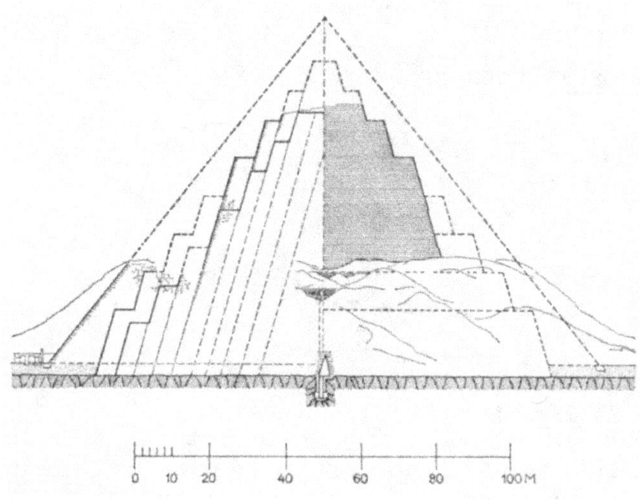

Structure: core, masonry and façade Source 4)

"One question: If I were a billionaire, would you build me a pyramid of Cheops today?"

"Such a planning contract would be fantastic" calls Sahin "but no, unfortunately I would have to turn it down."

The Cheops pyramid built today

If a billionaire wanted a Pyramid of Cheops today and commissioned the new construction, even the largest construction companies would swallow: 26 million stone blocks weighing 25 tons each. The stones would have to be brought in from quarries all over Europe.

It would take the companies involved an estimated 10 - 15 years to build using the most modern equipment.

The former Burj Khalifa construction site in Dubai would only be a small construction site in relation to the pyramid Source: Holydaycheck

But even before that, no renowned architect would take on the planning contract because he knows:
The structural engineering problems, especially the static problems that would arise during construction, are still unsolvable today!
This is mainly due to the gigantic size (see point 3.) and the resulting structural difficulties.

"The main difficulties that are still unsolvable today are the foundation, i.e. the weight and the associated statics to ensure that the building does not fall apart."

8. The structural facts

The core masonry of the Pyramid of Khufu consists of a calculated 16 million stones. In order to pile up this mass - the mass alone - of stones, regardless of the building hypothesis
- 11,45 years on 360 days (!)
- ten hours a day (!)
- every *seven minutes* (!)

a load of stones would have had to be pulled up every seven minutes (!) for 1145 years to complete the workload. This was calculated by a math professor. Source 4)

You should imagine this in practical terms: In a heat of 30 - 40 and more degrees in the shade that means 50 degrees and more in the sun (because there is no shade on the pyramids) and at the top of the pyramid even significantly more degrees, workers pull a stone of two and more tons up a ramp - however built - every seven minutes for almost 12 years, up to a height of the 50th floor of a skyscraper. Believable? Hardly.
A trained athlete climbed the Giza pyramid (without the stone) in 7 - 8 minutes, which means that all the (smaller and weaker) workers at the time would have had to literally run up the ramp with the two and a half ton

stone blocks in order to keep to the above construction time.

These stones would have had to be delivered in advance from the nearby quarry or from even further away and be ready.

Size comparison: The author and a stone lying on the ground, 2015

The aforementioned stonemason workers in the quarry may have worked most days of the year, but the farmers had to take care of agriculture every year after the flooding of the Nile in order to survive. They were hardly available to build pyramids during this time.
A quarry was found, but how should we imagine the work there?

Quarry Source: Pixabay.com

It is possible to chisel stone blocks out of such or similar stone layers by hand using simple tools, but it is time-consuming. First, starting from the top, the stone blocks have to be split into smaller pieces by cutting slits in the desired direction. Specially made wooden wedges then had to be hammered into these slits and moistened with water (from the Nile). This moistening of the wood creates a high swelling pressure because damp wood swells and expands, causing the stone to split.

The split stone could then be levered out of the stone structure using wooden poles and chipped to the right size with a mallet or, if necessary, split again or sawn into the right rectangular shape with a lot of patience and perseverance. Several men were needed for each stone and it took around 40 hours per stone to swell.
The stone now had to be brought to the pyramid to be ready for "transportation to the

top". The calculated mass of millions of stones weighing several tons was therefore probably not feasible at the time.

9. Previous building theories

Almost all relevant publications describe "building theories" for the construction of the pyramids. It is important to note that these are theories and not proven knowledge!

No one was present during the construction and no one has ever built a replica.

The following theories are the most popular for pyramid construction:

      1 The direct ramp
      2 The spiral ramp
      3 The machine theory
      4 The staircase theory

I have studied these theories in detail and would like to present them briefly:

1 The ramp theory

This well-known (erroneous) theory, which has been spread several times via television, assumes that the Egyptians built one or even four direct ramps that "grew" with the size of the pyramid. The workers are said to have used these ramps to pull the stones up to the finished level of the pyramid.

From a TV program with a misleading wooden box

"Green stuff on sand is no use for a sledge made of wood with a stone weighing tons," says Sahin, "for me the picture is a laughing stock because the sledge sinks completely with a real stone weighing tons on sand. Here in the picture it's an empty wooden box - that works in the movie but doesn't apply to the reality of the time."

Pulling a sledge sounds deceptively simple at first, but unfortunately only in theory:
If you assume a ramp has a gradient of *five percent*, which is already relatively steep here, to still have a length of *three kilometers* you have to have considerable pulling and pushing forces to move the weight forward.

There was no room for such a long ramp,

several kilometers long, in front of or next to the three great Egyptian pyramids.

"Not only was there no room for such a long ramp at the pyramids," says architect Sahin, "but the *annual Nile flood* would have washed it away every year. This influential theorist probably simply "overlooked" the required length and the important Nile flood."

The pyramids are too close together for a ramp. And at that time the ground level was about 10 meters lower than today, which means that any ramp would have had to be much steeper or longer.

Sketch:

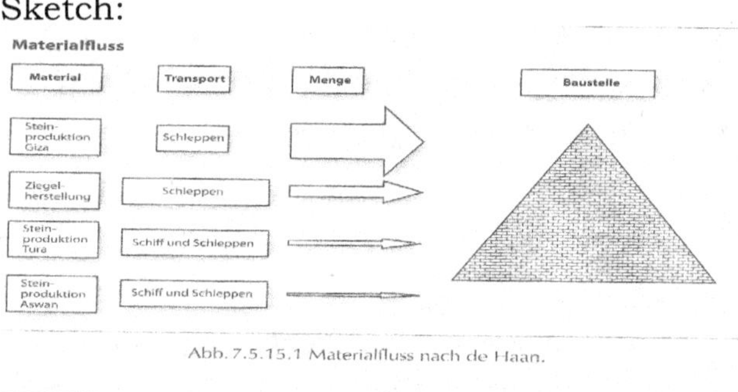

Abb. 7.5.15.1 Materialfluss nach de Haan.

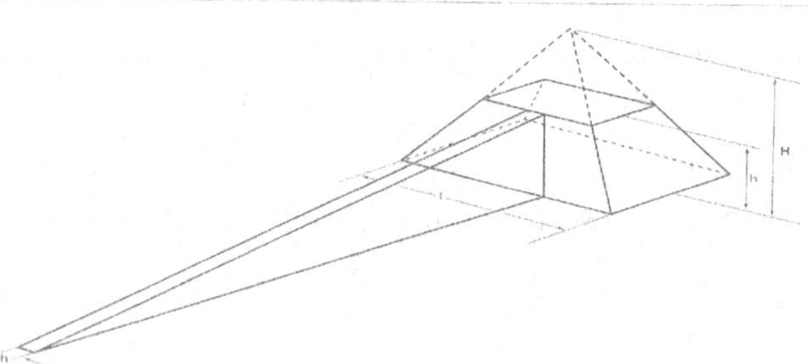

Theory of the ramp Source 4)

Pulling the stone blocks directly up onto the pyramid (as shown below) is also impossible for another reason, because the pulling weight cancels out the pulling force when a certain number of people are involved. A standard number is 20 people. A further 80 or 100 men (as shown below) will not increase the weight.

This is the effect known from the rope pulling game. The number of people pulling and pushing is therefore limited to relatively few people.

Only half of the following pullers (about 8 rows) can achieve a real conversion of the pulling force - all others are superfluous.

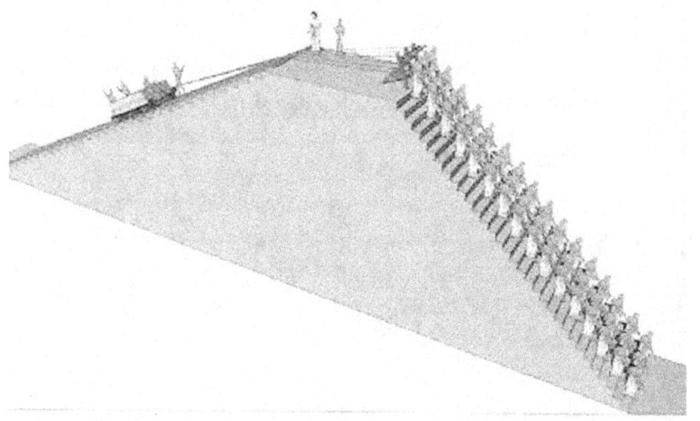

Abb. 8.2.1.3 Transport der Steine über eine drehbar angeordnete Umlenkwalze

Source 4)

It can therefore be seen that in this theory
- the weight
- the time
- the number of people pulling or pushing

persons and

- the result

do not fit together. So almost everything about this ramp theory is wrong:

Firstly, the angle of inclination of the pyramid steps (see point 3.) is too steep to walk on.

Secondly, the number of people pulling on the steps cancels out once a certain number is reached. More people do not have a higher pulling force. However, fewer people cannot transport the weight of the stones.

Thirdly: At the top of the pyramid there is a "large hole" in the middle for the burial chamber (follows), so the middle could not have been entered.

Fourthly, the rope would have had to be very, very long, i.e. longer than the conditions at the time.

"If there was a ramp," says Sahin, "there must have been at least four direct ramps, one from each side, because if the workers arrived at the top of the pyramid with a stone weighing several tons, they would have to turn the stone and insert it, which is impossible with just one ramp. Today this is done with a crane".

Scheme: 4 ramps one from each side
Missing: There is a large hole in the middle for the burial chamber and for access inside. And at the top there is a pyramidion (follows).

Architect Sahin has the following opinion on this:

"Further problems arise with the ramp theory in relation to.
- the ramp material
  the subsoil for the ramps
- the weight of the stones from about 2 tons
  per stone
- the transportation problem, i.e. moving the
  stones forward of the stones
- the arrangement on the pyramid and
- the height of the pyramid of around 50
  storeys.

Technicians have calculated that such a gigantic ramp would have required a volume of 20 million cubic meters - almost ten times more than the pyramid itself.

The ramp material

If we still assume a ramp, the next question is: What *material* was used for the ramp?

Option 1: Desert sand material

The obvious choice is to use desert sand from the surrounding area, which is desert.

Anyone who has ever climbed up a sand dune should have been busy enough with their own weight and the heat, because with every step you sink deep into the sand and slide back down again.

The architect comments:

"The desert sand is loose and does not solidify. Suppose you place a stone weighing two tons on this loose sand. You can see how it sinks into the desert sand.
Sand is therefore an unsuitable ramp material. Even if you put rollers and rails underneath. It doesn't solve the problem of loose sand. The workers would not be able to move a meter".

Those who subscribe to this theory can only be asked to prove it.

A sand dune consists of loose sand

Loose desert sand has no load-bearing capacity and is not suitable for building

Variant 2: Ramp material limestone chippings

Grit is denser than sand, but it would have to be
- first produced (1st step) and then
- then piled up (2nd step) and then compacted

- then compacted (3rd step)

to be able to bear the weight of the stone blocks. Today, this is done with heavy machinery (see photo below) which did not exist back then.

Due to its enormous mass and strength, this chippings material should still be found nearby today.

Earth can be compacted with loads, but this was and is rare in Egypt.

Earth also carries a heavy excavator

And the Nile mud was used for agriculture. In addition, the mud was soft, so it had to be dried first and was not available in the quantities that would have been needed for a ramp due to agriculture. Its strength for this purpose is also questionable.

Quarry, weight and shape of the stones

Scientists assume an average weight of 2,5 tons per stone with a volume of 1,2 m³ for the core masonry of the Pyramid of Cheops. According to calculations, it took 40 hours to split such a block of stone in the quarry. Added to this is the time needed to lever it out of the stone layer (with which tool?), which would have required several workers.

According to theories, the stones of the core masonry were broken out of the earth in a nearby quarry and worked in this way.

Possible appearance of a quarry in the evening sun Source: Pixabay.com

It cannot be said often enough. The tools of the time were only: axe or hammer shovel spade ropes and sledges made of (imported) wood for transportation. There were only tools made of wood or copper, but copper is a soft material. So was bronze.

However, the wheel had not yet been invented. The actual and strongest means of transporting loads at this time were animals (not machines).

There is no evidence of steel tools. Perhaps there were stone balls, i.e. round stones that could be used for transportation purposes, as a kind of predecessor to the wheel.

Photo from 1838 visible: Transportation of goods across the Nile *by camel,* better seen on our website.

The transportation of granite stones

Granite stones can also be found in the

pyramids and in scientific literature it is assumed that these were transported to Giza from the Aswan area by boat. Today this would not be a major problem, but I must refer again and again to the time 4500 years ago.

Back then, people went fishing with boats made of papyrus or wood. They used such boats to transport (import) agricultural products as well as wood and export their own products.

Naked fisherman on a papyrus boat of the time Source 2)

Were such light boats also suitable for transporting granite stones weighing several tons from quarries near present-day Aswan to the pyramids? "Experts" believe that stones and granite weighing several tons were broken out of the ground in Aswan and transported from the construction site on boats (see photo above) around a thousand kilometers downstream to the pyramids. Architect Sahin shakes his head at these words.

"I don't think this is generally possible for the following reasons:
Transporting stones weighing tons from the quarry to the Nile and loading them onto a boat using only human power is *not possible.* If it had been possible, the boats would have sunk from the weight".
The lack of human strength for such transports is proof that the transport of granite stones with these boats and in these masses over this length of around one thousand kilometers was *impossible* at the time.

Dangerous crocodiles and hippos also swam in the Nile. Shoals, sandbanks and waterfalls were also present. So many boats would have had accidents, but I don't think that the people of the time would have dared to take such a risk. In any case, no relevant dramas have survived.

Proponents of this theory should verify their unproven claims with tests or retract them.

Crocodiles still exist (2015) but no hippos

The arrangement of the stones at the top of the pyramid

If, despite everything, one assumes that there was a ramp, then its height would have had to be adjusted to the progress of construction during the building period.

Assuming an estimated 20 workers actually arrived at the top of the pyramid with a 25-ton stone - and now?
How can the stone be brought to the right place or into the right position?

Supposedly with stone balls, which were already known at that time. But you have to lift the stone block to get the stone balls underneath. Here, too, the question immediately arises: Lifting? At the top of the pyramid?

The top of the pyramid itself consists of a pyramidion weighing several tons.

The Cheops pyramid from above with pyramidion Source 2)

This should have been transported in the same way and it should have been placed "from above" - from the sky? What tools were used and where were the people standing?
In short: It was *impossible* to "set up" the pyramidion at that time and even today no helicopter could transport the pyramidion due to its weight in the air.

2 Theory: The spiral ramp

Even more absurd is another popular theory that assumes an outer ramp that was built around the pyramid similar to a spiral staircase.

To think about it: A square structure of limestone with a side length of 238,7 m (length about 40 terraced houses) is built, tapering towards the top, and a ramp with a width of say at least 6 meters (for two transport routes 1 x up and 1 x down) is filled with limestone or sand to pull up the above-mentioned stones weighing tons.

And the whole thing is built to a height of around 150 meters and then the ramp is removed again.

You can tell:
The inventor was a theorist! The theory cannot work in practice because, *in addition* to the above ramp theory, the following problems also arise:
* The pyramid to be built would be completely covered by the surrounding ramp.

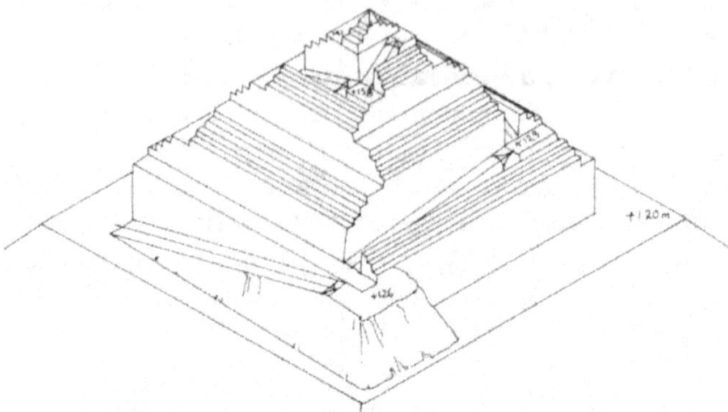

The spiral ramp drawing according to this theory
Source 4)

It would not be visible during construction. How would it then be possible to build it at an exact angle and evenly tapering upwards without today's technical aids if it could not be seen?
* The ramp would be several kilometers long after just a few circuits of the pyramid. An engineer*) has calculated that the clearing would have taken longer than the construction itself due to the mass.
*) Source 4)

* This means that there would still have to be gigantic spoil heaps in the vicinity.

* The construction would have consumed vast quantities of wood or other building materials, which would have had to be delivered from "somewhere".

Further ramp theories

There are also the following:

* Ramps running vertically towards the pyramid Proposals by Stadelmann Lauer Borchardt Lattermann Höhn.

* Lateral ramps Proposals by Goyon Lehner Klemm Graefe Hampikian Hölscher Petrie Houdin Willburger.

* Building hypotheses on the use of lifting and pulling devices Proposals by Isler Croon Löhner Santos Riedl Abitz Munt Dorka Pitlik Bormann Parry Keyssner Winkler Unterberger de Haan Hodges Source 4).

The architect's comment:
"All experts but not from construction."

3 The machine theory

Another theory states that the Egyptians built their pyramids with the help of machines. The Greek historian Herodotus already wrote about "machines" in the 5th century BC (presumably a misleading translation). In modern research, however, this possibility has already been rejected as workshops and work camps were found during excavations in the vicinity of the pyramids, but no evidence of machines that could have been used to lift and pull such loads.

"Real machines" were first used by the Greeks and Romans. So, in ancient Egypt, there should have been machines in the sense of leverage as they existed 2000 years later among the Greeks and Romans?

"Typical machines" still on the Nile today Source 2)

If so, then the question arises: What material was it made of? In other words: To lift a stone weighing approx. 25 tons that high, you need
a) a very hard material such as steel to support this weight as a construction and
b) an equally strong rope and
c) an appropriate counterweight
to bring it to the height of the top of the pyramid of up to 150 m (!).

I think this would only be possible today with a very large amount of thick steel girders - more powerful than in today's large buildings.

"The "machine idea" is completely absurd," says architect Sahin.

4 The staircase theory

The Institute of Egyptology at the University of Münster rejects ramps as an explanation: According to their own theory, the large pyramids such as that of Cheops would originally have had a structure in steps, just like smaller pyramids. Smaller steps are said to have been built into these steps and the blocks were lifted upwards over them. The question arises here too: With what material and with what tools?

Pyramids in the form of steps are not absurd, as there are many such pyramids.

Mayan pyramid in Mexico built with "portable" stones.

Pyramids in the form of stairs are not absurd because there are many of them. The staircase form is actually THE construction method for many pyramids outside Egypt, for example the Mayan pyramids in Mexico (see photo), which I have also visited, or for temples such as those in Iran, but these are other countries and above all other times, namely several thousand years later - and the temples are significantly lower!

This theory is therefore not applicable to the Giza pyramids. In any case, there is no evidence of a possible staircase construction because the pyramids look like stairs but are far too steep to be walked on (see point 2.).

The problem of stone transportation

The general problem with the pyramids is the stones and their transportation. A nice "stone portfolio":

Photo from Persepolis (Iran)

For the much smaller men of the time (as described above), stones as heavy as a centner (in hundredweights, not tons) as shown in the photo above must have been at the very limit of transport.

The staircase construction method was feasible at that time with stones up to a weight that "four strong men" could carry to a height of up to 20 meters. This was probably the case with the Mayan pyramids, for example. This is a characteristic of the construction of pyramids and temples in ancient times.

Some also believe that stones were transported in Egypt using a wooden stretcher.

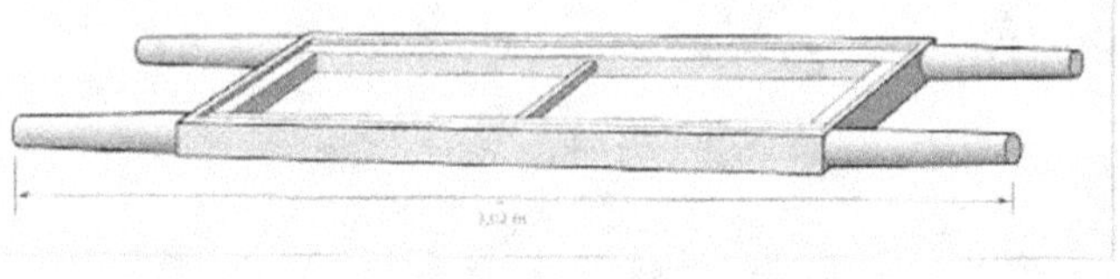

Transport tool wooden stretcher Source 4)

This also seems unlikely to me because how could one climb a pyramid with such a relatively lightly built stretcher with a heavy stone if ramps and stairs are out of the question?

Other step pyramids

There are the following other pyramids with stairs or steps in Egypt:

The Red Pyramid	Neferfre
Djedefre	Niuserre
Chephren	Menkauhor
Bicheris	Djedkare Asosi
Mykerinos	Unas
Userkaf	Lepsius
Sahure	Ibi
Neferirkare	Chui
Schepseskare	Amenemhet's I and II
	Sesostris' I II III

and many more smaller pyramids. (Source 4)

By the way: In the 3rd - 6th dynasty, i.e. over a period of around 470 years, construction began on 25 large pyramids!

No ramps no stairs

Back to the basic question of how the pyramids in Egypt were built. As the Egyptians themselves did not leave any descriptions or these have since been lost, the first person to do so is a certain Mr. Herodotus from Greece who visited Egypt in the 5th century BC, more than 2000 years later, and received information from priests about which he reported. For the construction of the pyramids, he writes of wooden scaffolding on which the stones were lifted from step to step and then:

"Thus first the top was finished then downward to the lowest steps." (Source 4)

This seems correct to me! But it contradicts itself in the case of a new building because you can't build the top (the roof) "in the air" first and then erect the walls. In my opinion, however, his report is absolutely correct!

The ultimate proof
against ramps or stairs

The ultimate proof that none of these ramp or

staircase hypotheses could ever work because the conditions were completely different is shown in the following photo from 1838:

The annual flooding of the Nile, which has not occurred since the Nasser Reservoir, i.e. since 1976, previously flooded the entire area on which the houses of Giza (over 4 million inhabitants), among others, stand today for thousands of years.

Clearly visible: The Nile flood almost reaches the pyramids (better to see in color on our homepage)

During this period of flooding, the Nile water apparently almost reached the pyramids.

If the pyramids had been built with ramps, they would have been washed away by the annual masses of water from the Nile! So no construction time of 20 years for thousands of workers.

This is the end of the dead end from which all earlier theorists can no longer escape.

Back to pyramid construction and the inside of the pyramid. Another difficulty is the burial chamber.

10. The interior of the pyramid: The burial chamber

All previous scientists and certainly also visitors are very impressed by the appearance of the inside of the pyramid.

The entrances the size of the gallery the plain room in which a granite sarcophagus stands up to the locking of the entrance with heavy granite slabs are impressive.

The pyramid has the following structure:

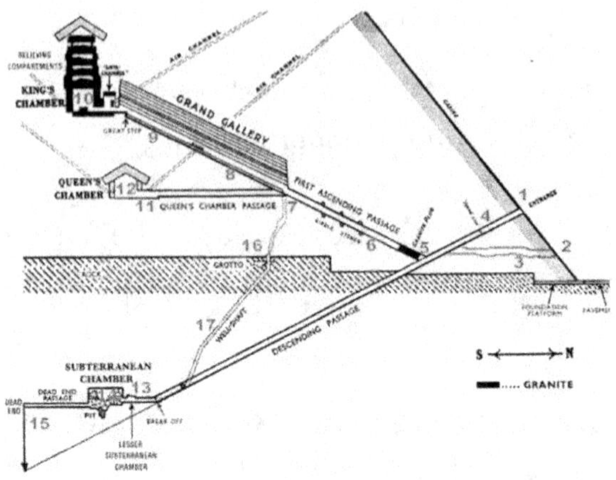

Sketch of the inner structure Source 5)
Main path: From entrance 1 first downwards from no.
5 upwards through the "Grand Gallery" to the King's
Chamber 10 or from no. 5 downwards.

Or a simpler drawing:

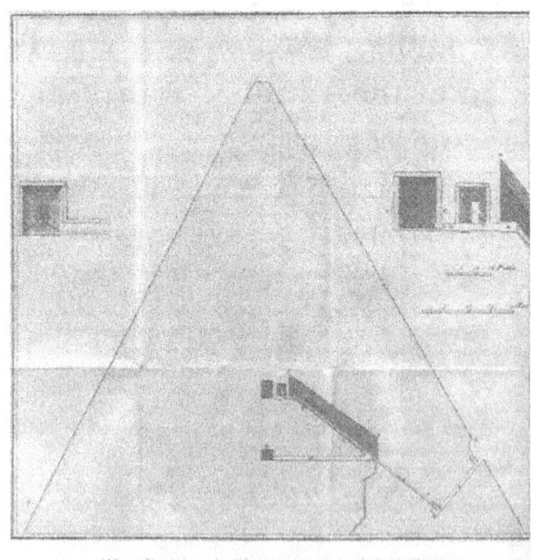

Abb. 2. Das Innere der Cheopspyramide (nach de Maillet 1740)

Source 5)

I have not found any real indications from previous authors as to how this interior of the pyramids was probably built. However, I noticed some unusual points during my visit in 2015:
- The corridors have certainly been subsequently smoothed and made "tourist-friendly" for masses of people.

Nice smooth walls trip-free floor 2015

- In the large gallery, newer iron struts have been installed - presumably for safety reasons - to prevent the wall panels from falling.
- In the Pharaoh's burial chamber, the

originally rough wall has been smoothed and covered with a modern rubbing plaster(!).

Architect Sahin smiles at this and says:

"No layman will notice the work has been done to the highest quality but a building expert won't miss it. At the same time, the joints have been tightened so that the wall now looks as if it consists of many large (square) stones.

However, this is almost a "backdrop construction" in terms of appearance. This type of coating has only recently been introduced. Burial chambers plastered in an ancient way can be seen in Luxor in the Valley of the Kings and these look completely different".

The Gallery, looking up 2015

The sarcophagus in the burial chamber

At the back wall of the (dark) burial chamber is a sarcophagus weighing several tons. One thing struck me as soon as I stood in front of it: after this crazy effort with the pyramid, is this ugly granite trough supposed to have been the pharaoh's tomb?

Sarcophagus in the pyramid of Cheops Source: Ägypt. Museum

Also:

The granite is *perfectly polished* on the inner and outer walls. With which tools would it have been possible to grind granite, the hardest stone on earth (known as paving stone in the old towns of Western Europe), smooth by hand on the outside and four inner walls?

The inner walls of the sarcophagus are perfectly carved, but the upper edge is chipped or damaged all around. The room is empty and - as already mentioned - plastered "smooth and modern" with today's plaster.

One should bear in mind:
Granite has been known since Roman times as a hard-wearing hard floor covering. This granite trough in the Pyramid of Cheops could therefore not possibly have been worked in this way around 4,500 years ago with the soft wooden tools of the time, at most copper, and delivered to this location.

If the sarcophagus was a tomb of the Pharaoh Cheops, the following questions arise:
* How could the sarcophagus and the mummy with transported to this height with the priests transported to this height?
* How could the usual death ceremonies be carried out at this height?
* There is said to have been a secret side entrance but this does not solve the problem of the height.
* Furthermore, in my opinion the sarcophagus does not fit at all with a ruler who saw himself as "god-like". The trough looks like a foreign body, and it is.
* How did it get to this place in the first place?

All the burial chambers of the pyramids were looted anyway and - I'm sure - all the burial chambers have been "reworked" over the past 4500 years. The way you see them today is not the original state. There were already many at work (see next nr. 11).

I suspect that in much later times, when the Arabs or even later the French or the English occupied Egypt, the trough was pulled up on behalf of a "crazy stranger" using strong ropes and technical equipment of the time (winches, steel cables etc.). When it reached the top, it was pushed on rollers to its current position and the unknown client lost interest. Or it was actually buried there and was stolen along with everything else. Tourists have also severely damaged the trough (follows).
It now stands damaged in the empty chamber for tourists to view for an entrance fee.

11. Interventions, Destruction, Tourists

There are certainly big differences between the state of today and the original state of that time. In the long history of Egypt, many people have been very "actively" involved with the pyramids. Many treasures can be seen in museums around the world, especially in Germany, England, France and the USA. All of these originals were "taken" from the site in Egypt and transported to distant countries.

There is a suspicion that unfortunately (too) many people were involved in the construction of the pyramid. As a result, the original condition was considerably altered. Professor Erhard Oeser has taken the trouble to publish what was previously written about the pyramids in a book (source 5).

And indeed, the Greeks, the Romans, the Arabs, the French and the English were already actively at work and this is "only" the last 2000 years.

Very briefly:

1 The Arab period

There must have been an open entrance for a long time. Then it was closed again and a named caliph broke in and found "*a marble hollow that was closed with a lid. When the lid was removed, he found only rotten bones inside*".

Since the pyramid was open, a pyramid tourism apparently developed because many people were enthusiastic and could not be stopped from visiting the pyramid and descending into it through the slippery passageway - some remained intact while others died. Source 5)

Another named Arab and alleged eyewitness reports the pyramid as a mass grave in which several bodies lay covered with a large number of shrouds. None had white hair and the bodies were strongly built (meaning they were not old when they died).

Abb. 3 Die Araber in der großen Galerie
(nach Luigi Mayer 1805)

Arabs in the large gallery Source 5)

2 The French

In 1395 AC, a named Frenchman reported that he witnessed quarrying work at the Great Pyramid. When asked, he was told "that for 1000 years almost all the beautiful buildings in Cairo have been built from such stones".
Today it is assumed that the missing stones from the pyramids were used to build houses in Cairo.

Around 1500 AC, another Frenchman reported a chest in the royal chamber made of black marble in one piece and without a lid or contents. And at the end of the great hall they found a well shaft filled with stones and realized that water had once been drawn from it.

Around 1580 AC, two other Frenchmen dared to climb to the top of the pyramid and - with a torch in their hands - they entered the interior of the pyramid through a square opening.
They also came across a well, but it was not blocked with rubble and debris. They threw several stones into it, which "only echoed after half an hour, from which they concluded that it must be very deep". They also found a chest without a lid or contents and broke off a piece of the trough out of curiosity.

3 Frenchman de Maillet and Napoleon

The much-traveled French diplomat Benoit de Maillet visited the pyramids around 1680 A.D. and discovered that the pyramid's façade had been finished and subsequently opened by force.

And he drew up a plan of the pyramid. Inside, deep holes had been cut in the corridors and everything was dark and blackened by smoke from the tallow candles and candles. Overall, he noticed a lot of damage.

"Heavy traffic" on the pyramid Source 10)

In 1798 Napoleon began the war with Egypt and founded an "Institute for Science and the Arts" in Cairo, which was to focus on researching the pyramids, which it did.

Engineer Jomard doubted whether the pyramid was intended as a burial place because it is not proven whether "any king was ever buried there". Source 5)

Napoleon and the pyramids Source 5)

4 The British colonization

After the French came the British, who initially supported an Italian captain who also entered the pyramid.
"With the torch, they discovered smoke-blackened crude Latin characters on the ceiling that were barely legible but proved that this room was open at the time of the Romans".

He dug another passage but made no progress.

A British officer finally managed to open up a passage by blasting it with *gunpowder*.

This happened even more often, with gunpowder being used to clear the way to the relief chambers above the King's Chamber.

Around 1849 AD, an "Egyptomania" broke out in Great Britain. People carelessly fired pistols and muskets around the chambers and narrow corridors to chase away bats and listen to the many echoes. Huge blasts were carried out in search of new hidden rooms and even pieces of the sarcophagus in the king's chamber were taken away as souvenirs.

By 1860 AD there must have been a veritable stream of tourists through the pyramids. Equipped with candles, they walked through the interior of the pyramids shouting "hurrah". These first photographs show the flow of tourists:

Egyptomania: tourists around 1800 Source 10)

Japanese and other tourists

Drawing from 1823

It is striking that the landscape looks considerably different each time. This is particularly noticeable in the first photos from the mid-1800s.

The Sphinx around 1800

It is easy to see here and also conceivable that the annual flooding of the Nile often reached as far as the neck of the Sphinx so that the whole area below was under water every year.

Water damage to the neck of the Sphinx

Giza photo around 1800 Source 10)

Conclusion so far:

It was natural to assume that the pyramids would often attract attention in the following millennia, but the excavations and demolitions that were carried out were already very violent changes. There is also a well that was filled with water and then again with stones and rubble. The trough in the burial chamber was also found without and then again with damage.

The entrance to the interior was repeatedly opened and closed and then broken open again. And officially nothing was found except "a few rotten bones".

Later, "many corpses" were said to have been lying in the pyramid, but no one found any treasures. If there were any, then these treasures were stolen by grave robbers before the Greeks and Romans - more than 2000 years ago.

The use of stones from the pyramids for the construction of houses in Cairo also represents serious irreparable damage to an ancient work of art.

**The building hypotheses to date
can be summarized as follows:**

31 scientists (plus unknown ones) since the period from 1800 AD onwards have dealt extensively with the construction of the pyramids. The theories come from people with different educational backgrounds and professions, but they all have one thing in common: They assume a new building and they hardly have any construction or real estate-specific expertise, especially not for large-scale projects. And they assume technical progress that the indigenous peoples of the time could not have achieved in terms of evolution.

There is not the slightest indication that there was such a surge in inventions, technology, know-how, etc. at this time and only here in this small area around Memphis that such gigantic pyramids could have been erected for the first time in a relatively short time.

And just as suddenly, all this knowledge and expertise disappears into the desert sands without leaving any trace? That is extremely unlikely.

The scientists mentioned also have the following in common: they were unable to offer a viable, real-life solution! Earlier people always created projects that were close to life.

So the question is: can so many scientists be wrong? Yes! Even the Roman Seneca said: "Where everyone is going is not necessarily the right way".

"That's right!" says Sahin. "The people mentioned all have one thing in common: they are competent in their field and have found out a lot about the time, but *when it comes to building, you should ask construction experts.*"

The construction of the pyramids is the focus of this book. It should have become clear that so far there have been no satisfactory answers as to how they were built. My impression is that it was simply not possible to explain how the pyramids were built. And that's why people have tried to "somehow" theoretically explain the basically untenable theories or link them to "mysteries and miracles".

The theories mentioned remind me in principle of a process that I know well from the real estate sector: a property developer advertises, for example, that project XY will yield a "return of x%". All those involved (the sales department, the bank, etc.) then use various formulas to calculate the specified return instead of saying that this return is not possible.

And it's the same with pyramid building. In my opinion, these theories are a completely wrong approach. Architect Sahin comments:

"Building a pyramid of this size today, that is, in 2023, is still not possible, as I said before. This is due to the physical conditions of our planet. We will talk about this later."

If you want to rebuild pyramids from the bottom up, you should first study the *principles of construction*. This will now take place.

12. Principles of building

When building, you generally have to adhere to certain principles that apply all over the world and were also valid 4500 years ago. The larger the construction project, the more important these principles are. They are as follows:

1 The initiator (builder)

The figure of Cheops very small Source Egypt. Museum

Whoever wants to build is called the builder. According to tradition, this was probably Cheops, the pharaoh-king. Not much is known about him.

He was the 2nd king in the 4th dynasty, reigning from around 2579 to 2556 BC.

He (but basically his people) bore the costs of the project. This was probably already the case at the time. Whether and in what form those involved received remuneration for their work is not known. Coins - i.e. money - have not been found, so payment, if there was any, may have been in kind. Some also believe that Khufu was a dictator and tyrant who forced his people to carry out the construction work. Even then, it was probably a mix of power, religion, praise and punishment.

2 The architect - master builder

Every major project needs an architect, also known as a master builder.

"A master builder has been recorded for the Cheops pyramid," says Sahin, "namely Vizier Hemiun (the highest-ranking official second to the king). This position of trust was only given to princes. His duties were all practical leadership tasks. Hemiun is the Pharaoh's nephew and my real "star" of the pyramid. More on this later.

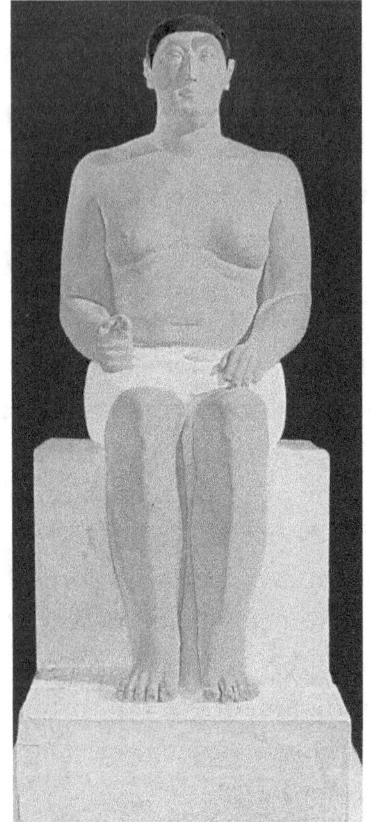

Hemiun the "pyramid genius" Source 1)

Up to this point, there has been nothing noticeable, but now come the crucial points.

3 The foundation

"Every new building needs a foundation. It is built as a stable straight surface that compensates for unevenness in the terrain and bears the weight so that the building does not break apart. It must therefore be very stable" Sahin says.

Today, deep foundations are built for this purpose. The larger the building, the deeper and thicker the foundation must be for structural reasons in order to support the tons of weight of a building.

Example: A small foundation in Germany

"But the pyramids have no foundations!" says the architect "and before you can build walls, you need at least a stable straight surface as a basic condition. and that doesn't exist".
Earlier theorists had already recognized this and for such a straight surface to build the first row of stones of the pyramid, for example, the filling of this row of stones with water was mentioned. A "great idea" with a coarse-grained sand-lime brick that immediately absorbs the water.

In addition, due to the extreme heat, a lot of water would have to be pumped into the rows of bricks in a short space of time - similar to a river. This would have required large pumps because, as already mentioned, the pharaoh's site is much higher above the Nile.

And then all this water would have had to be directed in such a way that a flat surface was created and at the same time the water somehow disappeared again. There is no indication of how this could have worked back then.

If there is no foundation, then a rock could also take over this function, as was the case with the Mayan pyramids in Mexico, for example. But the three pyramids in Egypt do not stand on any rock - there are none there that could support such a weight.

4 Static functions - the most important

"Statics is one of my favorite topics," says Sahin the architect, suddenly wide awake.
If a new building more than one meter high is to be built from the ground upwards, there must first be a foundation, as mentioned above. The load-bearing components (walls,

pillars, columns) are then erected on top of this and connected with cross bracing.

"So if the pyramids had been rebuilt from the bottom up, they would have been a *building*! And *a building needs statics* to prevent it from falling over or collapsing. The height is also a decisive criterion" I say.

In any case, certain walls in buildings have to perform static functions. That's why they have to be solidly built and connected to each other.

In a building as large as the pyramid, these walls or pillars would have to be *meters thick*! Even thicker than the columns of the temples in Luxor, for example. They would also have to be very close together, for example a pillar every few meters, similar to Stonehenge in England. They would be impossible to overlook".

Stonehenge, England, source Pixabay.com

"There should have been about 100 of them in the Cheops pyramid," says Sahin, "in the middle up to over 130 meters high, so stable that they could not topple over themselves and thus would not cause the pyramid to collapse. However, there is no evidence of statics in the pyramid - there is no structure that performs this important static function, because this statics should still be present unchanged. Columns only appeared later, from the 5th dynasty onwards".

That is impressive:
A 50-storey high and 40 townhouses wide structure newly built at that time without a built foundation even without rocks and without static components? That is - even today - an *impossibility*.

The weight of the Pyramid of Khufu is estimated at millions of tons and there are no pillars or beams! That should make you wonder: How can such a huge mass of stone without statics remain standing at all and survive the millennia without cracking?

In short: The "Cheops Colossus" without any statics?

5 A construction plan

Architect Sahin says:

"You need a construction plan for every major new building because many technical principles have to be adhered to, especially about statics and other structural specifications. These are always written down and everyone involved in the construction can see them to minimize errors.
This plan or drawings is usually drawn up by an architect or a master builder.

In Egypt, there are no wall drawings or writings (hieroglyphics) from this period - both were only at the beginning of development. It was not until 1000 years later that hieroglyphs on the walls of the temples showed processes and things that seemed important to those living at the time and to preserve them for posterity. However, no drawings or writings from the construction of the pyramids have yet been found, although the construction of each pyramid took an estimated 20 years. Every master builder would have made sure that the construction was permanently recorded in drawings and writings so that it could be completed without him after his possible death in the meantime because the average lifespan at that time was only around 30 years. Childhood and old age are deducted from the active lifetime.

But there is no blueprint and no "notes".

Perhaps they were not written in stone but in papyrus and the papyrus disintegrated. Or it was destroyed because Alexander the Great destroyed almost all the collected knowledge of the Egyptians in the 4th century BC. And in Caesar's time, according to tradition, the remaining books containing the "knowledge of the ancients" were burned in the Library of Alexandria.

Be that as it may, it remains to be said that there are no construction reports of the six pyramids built at this time.

"Perhaps they were not necessary because the building was understandable to the Egyptians of the time anyway?" says the architect.

6 The practical organization

Such a large pyramid construction site naturally requires good organization. According to the above-mentioned theories, between 20,000 and 30,000 people (assumptions vary widely) are said to have worked constantly on each pyramid. Practical implementation would therefore have required

- A large store for shovels axes ropes etc.
- Several large kitchens with pots, pans and containers

- Several tons of food per day
- Several hectoliters of drinking water daily
- Large toilet facilities
- Large halls for sleeping and resting
- A large hospital to care for the injured
etc.

A relatively small workers' camp and workers' graves have been located. Also a cemetery. Above all, however, the mass transportation of all the above necessities to a remote desert seems to me to be an unbelievable task at the time and, under these climatic conditions, hardly feasible for these masses of workers. Even this construction site equipment would have taken many years.

It would have required an incredible number of boats and skids with donkeys as well as camel transports through the desert every day to bring in these masses of food and drink. And all the people on the construction site? There must not have been so many thousands of able-bodied men and women working 365 days a year at that time! It must therefore have been a less strenuous construction method.

Conclusion:

* The most important prerequisites for a *new building* are missing.

* Without plans, it is not possible to build such a large project as a new building because the construction takes a very long time, i.e. at least two generations. The next generation must know how the construction is to continue.

* Underneath the pyramids there is no foundation, no rock structure for the stability that is essential for a new building.

* Without a structural network with walls, beams, supports, etc., such a large-scale project will inevitably collapse immediately or within a very short time.

Result:

* The pyramids could not have been erected from the bottom up like a new building because everything necessary for this was missing. Any theory of this kind is sheer nonsense.

* The pyramids are *not a new building* and therefore not a building. Not real estate.

So the question is: What then?

13. Nature builds

Many shapes and constructions in the world were not "built" by humans but by nature. There are many photos of formations around the world. It is not only man who builds, nature has also built its own wonders in the course of evolution.

Stone formation in the desert of Namibia

Rectangular (basalt) stones of a mountain in Iceland "built" by nature

Essential: Table mountains

Nature consists not only of plains mountains lakes but there are also many special mountains, so-called table mountains for example:

Striking table mountains in a desert

A single mountain stands out from a relatively flat surface. This is called a table mountain.

Table mountains were formed millions of years ago through evolution. The best known are certainly the "three pillars" in the USA, Table

Mountain in Cape Town/South Africa, Ayers Rock in Australia and many others.

Mesas in monument valley USA

From Giza along the Nile for around 1000 kilometers to the area where Lake Nasser is located today, there are several hundred table mountains in different shapes and sizes. Example:

"We have about hundreds of unnoticed mesas along the Nile," says Sahin, "unnoticed because they are part of nature.

So it is very likely that the pyramids were also natural mesas BEFORE".

The terrain behind the pyramids confirms this:

Terrain behind the pyramids 2015
The structure of a mesa is clear.
That is why the pyramids are so large.

14. The pyramid story

Table Mountain is also the answer to the question: Why is such a dominant structure as the pyramid (of all things) located in this place in a lonely desert far away from the capital and the people?

1 The location

Or to put it another way: why did a "god-like" pharaoh build his tomb not near his people in Memphis but 28 kilometers away and thus in a place in the desert that was six hours' walk away at the time, i.e. in a no-man's land?

Even back then, being king or pharaoh had a lot to do with "power" - you had to be a "man of power" who wanted to rule over everyone. And that a man of power who, according to the beliefs of the time, would return to earth from the darkness and then arrive in no man's land; such a thought would certainly have been unthinkable for a pharaoh even then, unless there was an extremely important reason for it. And this was due to the huge dimensions and the radiant power of the sun (follows).

So it is clear to me:
The location was not planned. At the site of the pyramid, there were *three huge mesas* that could be seen *far into the country*. And that is why the pyramids also stand in this place. This is how the location came about. And there were no alternatives for a large pyramid.

Three table mountains became three pyramids source Fotalia.com

2 The arguments

Now please follow me with the following thoughts:

Assuming that there was a table mountain where each of the pyramids stood, then

- it was not necessary to build a foundation
  build

- it was not necessary to carry tons of stones
  to carry up

- the pyramid has hardly any cracks even
  today because it is a natural stone material

- there is no need for elaborate new construction planning because the object was already there

- nothing was written down about the pyramid construction because the construction itself was "nothing special" for the people at that time just work, and that over two or more generations.

This is a *real-life situation* that was *feasible* for the first people with the tools of the time.

3 My Cheops story

In Ancient Egypt, barques played a major role in navigating the Nile.

Reconstructed Cheops barque in the museum on the south side of the Pyramid of Cheops
Source: www.benben.de

The royal barque was equipped with a simple pole at the front and back, which had a cultic or mystical meaning.

Now I say to architect Sahin:

"Every project has a back story and my favorite one is this:

Let's say King Cheops invited his nephew Hemiun for a boat trip on the Nile. So they went along the Nile in his 40-meter-long royal barge and in front of the (largest) mesa he said to him:

"*See this mountain in it shall be my grave.*"
And Hemion gulped and said:
"*In this great mountain?*"
"*Yes, it corresponds to my heavenly greatness and it will show me the way to the sun.*"
"*But we have to make the mountain a little more beautiful.*"

"Yes, it should be a pyramid like the one in Saqqara, only much bigger and more beautiful."
Hemion was amazed: *"That's not so easy."*
"Come up with something, I want to see a pyramid."

Inspired by the first pyramids in Saqqara and the newly invented construction method using stones, as well as the idea of a huge pyramid shining yellow in the sun and red at sunset, King Cheops may have come up with this idea and commissioned his vizier Hemiun to build it - and he was not disappointed.

4 Master builder Hemiun

Master builder Hemiun was certainly a handsome figure, a scholar, a kind of professor with a lot of charisma, the opposite of the usual gaunt people. He probably had a brown complexion (slightly colored in the following photo) and black or grey hair.
(see next page)

He could certainly be described as a genius and his intelligence was the basis for the pyramid.

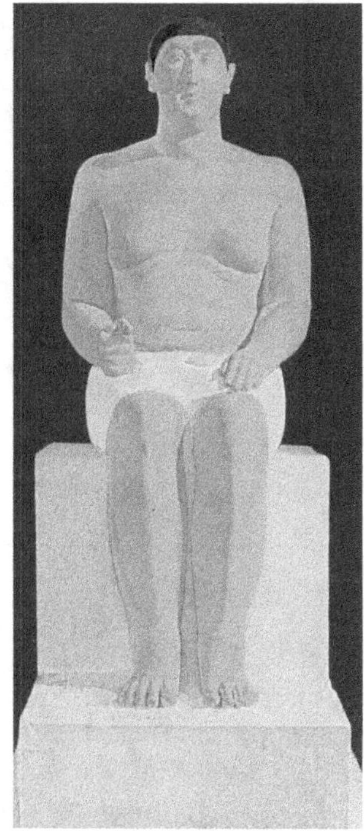

"Pyramid genius" Hemiun
Roemer and Pelizaeus Museum Hildesheim Source 1)

5 The building organization

The master builder Hemiun was clear: to manage such a project, you need clever employees and a very good organization with at least the following people:

- Administrative officials for the payment of all costs
- Architect and technician for the design
- Project manager on site to organize the

workers

- personnel manager for recruitment and
  catering.

These were just the managers from the upper echelons of society as well as many other people for:

- material store
- canteen kitchen
- Transportation of food and beverages
- Toilet facilities (waste disposal facilities)
- sleeping facilities
- Hospital and care of the injured
- Cemetery and burial of dead workers

and a large number of workers in the quarry and on the scaffolding (follows).

In order to manage all this, all able-bodied people in the empire were certainly involved.

6 The working method

However, it should not be assumed that there was a plan and a kind of "project start" (one whistle and off you go). Such a way of working only emerged during industrialization. There was a start, of course, but very slowly. People are lazy and comfortable by nature - then as now (this is not an accusation, just a realization). There was also no concept of time in today's sense (after all, the clock was only invented around 3000 years later), there was only the sun rising and setting every day, the weather was always the same and the Nile flooded. Everything therefore moved very slowly, as it still does today.

And the (positive) principle of achieving the greatest possible success with the least possible effort certainly applied to all craftsmen back then too. In other words: only as much effort as necessary, especially when the pay was certainly "poor" or nonexistent. The aforementioned heat should also not be forgotten.

Workers at the pyramids in 2015

"Our mentality," says Sahin, "was then and still is to sit together in a group and drink tea before starting work and to discuss all topics in detail and calmly".

So this must have been the case back then too, because it fits in with human nature.

Running up a kilometer-long steep path with stones weighing tons *in seven minutes* (according to the theories mentioned) and doing so in hot temperatures and 10 hours a day for years; such ideas are completely absurd.

15. The formation of the pyramids

The aforementioned Hemiun is known by name as the master builder of the Cheops pyramid. I therefore assume that he was commissioned by King or Pharaoh Cheops to build a pyramid for him according to the above story.

"Today's architects," says Sahin, "like to assume a "grand plan" for a project of this kind. But this was probably not the case. Not because no plan has yet been found, but because it was not necessary. The project was already in front of the workers for all to see.

* Learning by doing
I know it from renovating old buildings: you have a stone wall in front of you and don't know what will happen or come out when you want to change the wall. "Learning by doing" is what we call it today. It was probably similar for Hemion, but on a much larger scale. He had a really huge mountain in front of him. Maybe something like this:

Or maybe like this?

Or maybe like this?

Huge mesa - here is my "model mountain"

"His genius," Sahin begins, "was to think in dimensions that were still unknown at the time and to be able to put unprecedented things into practice. Let's put ourselves in his shoes:

In front of him stood a huge mesa. The inside was unknown. The structure of the mountain, the type of rock, etc. can hardly be seen from the outside. You never know what will happen next while you are working.

His genius was his approach. You have to assume that the ground level at that time was around 10 meters lower than it is today (so the pyramid at that time was also around 10 meters higher than it is today).

The fundamental question was: How do I approach the project of turning *a table mountain into a pyramid?*"

"You have to be able to imagine Table Mountain as a pyramid from above without having to climb it because it's too steep for that," I say.

"Yes," added the architect, "he certainly had a graphic memory and already imagined Table Mountain as a finished pyramid. That was the goal.

I'm sure he proceeded step by step during the realization.

1 First step: the pyramid shape as a template

Master builder Hemiun's first ingenious step was to erect a scaffold, presumably made of cedar wood, on the mountain as a template.

It should be remembered that this planned pyramid was 'uncharted building territory'. Although Hemiun may have been familiar with the pyramids from Saqqara (south of the then capital Memphis), this mesa in Giza had a completely different dimension as it was more than twice as high as the pyramid in Saqqara.

According to tradition, cedar wood up to 40 meters long was sufficiently strong and was imported. Straight scaffolding could be made from it and joined together four times to reach the height.

Erecting and aligning cedar poles on Table Mountain

"These poles had to be set up exactly at right angles as a triangle. Starting from these poles, the pyramid shape was feasible.

The pyramid shape on the table mountain - as an idea

2 Second step: The outer scaffolding
  and exact alignment

For a long time, I wondered how the "dead straight" alignment of the pyramids could be created by hand at an exact angle to each other. I saw the solution by chance on a building site in Persepolis in Iran. Later also at a current building site in Saqqara.

The means for this are quartz stones made from the quartz sand of the desert. These were used as so-called sun mirrors. With the help of the sun, the outer scaffolding was first aligned exactly straight while standing on the ground (the sun's rays are absolutely straight) and such a light signal is visible over many kilometers, i.e. in each case for the length of one side of the pyramid.
It must have taken a long time and many attempts before this was achieved. But time did not (yet) play a role.

Cedar poles at the exact angle

This outer scaffolding ultimately had to be extended about 4 times in height (4x 40 meters each including overlap).

3 Third step: internal scaffolding

Internal scaffolding was then attached to the external scaffolding and connected to the external scaffolding to achieve stability.

"For structural reasons," says the architect, "two types of scaffolding were needed: Internal and external scaffolding. The *inner scaffolding* was also important for the work on the pyramid in order to achieve the sloping pyramid shape. For this purpose, measuring marks were attached to them or extra poles with measuring marks. These showed the workers whether and how much mining material had to be removed to achieve the pyramid shape.

Standing on the scaffolding, the workers used

a wooden hammer or a spade to "knock down" the stones from the mesa up to the mark.

Typical wooden hammer to knock off stones

A current example:

Renovation scaffolding on a pyramid in 2015:
The outer scaffolding on the left (with man) the inner scaffolding to the right

This mosque in Isfahan is also a good example of interior and exterior scaffolding.

Example of exterior and interior scaffolding
at the mosque in Isfahan (Iran)

Today, such scaffolding is part of everyday life, but at the time this idea was ingenious.

Diagram: System of external and internal scaffolding

4 Fourth step: The rough pyramid shape

"After master builder Hemiun had inspected the scaffolding - slowly, deliberately and thoroughly - and approved it, he released it to the builders" Sahin says.

They climbed up the scaffolding *to the top* of the mesa and used their wooden, stone and copper tools to cut the mesa stones and the natural mountain material *from above* along the scaffolding to create a rough pyramid shape.

Wooden scaffolding on a pyramid in 2015

The chipped stone mass was lowered *down* in chutes. This answers the general question of transportation. Chutes could be built and anchored relatively easily *from top to bottom* using the usual basket material. The excavated rock could be crushed and - following the force of gravity - slid downwards. And from there it could be removed into the desert in baskets and on sledges.

This was heavy but in principle simple work that any man could do. No particular "high speed" was required to carry out the work and, again, no "tens of thousands of workers" were needed, which was also not insignificant for the supply of food and drink.

Coarse friable rock material in the pyramid area

Chipping away at the existing rock material in the heat was hard work, but even then it was still feasible, mainly for men.

The organization of the work

For this work from top to bottom, far fewer workers were needed than previously assumed. At the top of the scaffolding, there was only room for a few workers anyway and the number of workers increased towards the bottom.

There were probably experienced workers and stonemasons, i.e. specialists, for more difficult stone work. It is quite conceivable that Hemiun founded a "building school", i.e. a training center for the craftsmen.

I imagine the following three-part organization for the work on the pyramid:

* The top row of workers chipped the stone and the natural mountain material - they were the "*stone knockers*."

* Below them on the scaffolding were the "*clearers*" who lowered the rubble down the chutes.

* At the foot of the pyramids stood the "*carriers and transporters*" who removed the rubble from the building site.

The division of labor "in a team" is the oldest way of working since the existence of mankind.

Renovation scaffolding 2015;
in the Old Kingdom at the Pyramid of Khufu:
Stone breakers, clearing and transporting
among themselves

Division of labor and breaks

This division of labor into three stages was ingenious and simple at the same time and therefore the workers could easily be assigned to the respective group.

The workers were also able to take turns in this heavy physical work in the heat. It is also likely that the different groups (stone breakers, clearers and transporters) alternated or were assigned accordingly by a project manager. It is quite conceivable that master builder Hemiun was the first time that a very flexible system of division of labor was practiced in this almost serial form in the construction industry. This was sensational as a construction technique at the time, but obviously not unusual for the people (which is why nothing was written down).

Pyramid workers 2015: Hurry, Tempo and Time are foreign words

The pyramidion

The pyramid also includes the upper tip called the pyramidion. It is basically proof that the pyramid was not rebuilt from the bottom up because the pyramidion was not structurally possible for two main reasons:

* There would have had to be a ramp or staircase leading to a height of over one hundred and fifty meters. But ramp and stairs are fundamentally ruled out, as already described.

* According to calculations, the pyramidion weighs several tons. This cannot be

transported to the fiftieth floor using purely human strength.

(This quickly becomes apparent if, for example, a washing machine - weighing only about fifty kilograms - had to be transported by hand up the stairs to the fiftieth floor).

The pyramidion must therefore also have originally belonged to the table mountain and it was formed into this shape at the top. It was certainly the most difficult work and the difficulty lay above all in the even right-angled shape so that the top was straight. It must have taken many attempts before this was finally achieved.

Pyramidion of the Chephren pyramid Source 2)

The scientists write that the pyramidion was "set down" - from above? From the air? No, it was already there as a mesa and was *formed* into a pyramidion.

Let us now put ourselves in Hemiun's position.

After this processing step, he was faced with a huge mountain that somehow looked "unattractive", at least far from the ideal line. Holes and overhangs resulted from the rock material of the mountain. Four diagonal walls in the shape of a triangle were now required.

5 Fifth step: the masonry

Still standing on the scaffolding, the next step was to shape the "roughly formed mountain" into a "beautiful" and above all uniform (pyramid) form, just as King Cheops and his master builder wanted.
The coarse natural mountain material of the table mountain, i.e. holes and protrusions, had to be evened out in order to achieve an exact, clear and even pyramid shape.

Rectangular or square stones were now required. Suitable stones were available in the nearby quarry. There they were broken out by hand using simple tools and worked manually as described under point 7 Quarry.
From a constructional point of view, there must therefore have been close cooperation between the workers on the scaffolding and the specialists (stonemasons) in the quarry.

There they were carried up to the pyramid (in portable size) or transported by animals.

"At the beginning of the project," the architect says, "when the respective transport arrived at the pyramid, only the roughly hewn mesa stood in front of them. In order to achieve the exact right-angled pyramid shape, the accuracy of the first rows of stones was particularly important. They were lined up on the ground along the existing poles of the outer framework and aligned, presumably using the same method of sun and quartz sandstones as described.

The next stones were then added layer by layer, interlocked with each other and structurally aligned with the "Table Mountain".

The masonry of the Pyramid of Khufu is based on the (now invisible) Table Mountain behind it.

The masonry - stones of a sustainable size

"Further up," the architect continues his speech, "the stones had to be pulled up one by one with ropes by the workers standing on the scaffolding and inserted one on top of the other.

Or they were made on the spot from the core masonry of Table Mountain and inserted directly into the stone formation.

There were certainly not only workers but also "technicians" who were part of the management team. They reported to the quarry what was needed on the mountain and the exact shape of the stones required."

So there must have been intensive cooperation and "interaction". After all, these stones are decisive for the uniform shape of the pyramid on which the façade was then attached in the next step.

"The important thing," says architect Sahin, "is that these stones, which are clearly visible today, are part of the masonry of the "first cladding" of the rough mesa. They were probably piled on top of each other *from bottom to top* and leaned against the mesa".

The following close-up clearly shows the piled-up stones of the masonry.

Above all, they are of a size that could be carried by two to four "strong men".

Breaking these stones out of the nearby quarry, knocking them into the right shape with a wooden hammer, spade and (copper) chisel, transporting them to the scaffolding and lifting them up with ropes - probably in several stages - must have been the hardest and most tedious work on the pyramid.

In my opinion, this masonry is the reason for the construction theories mentioned (ramp, stairs, etc.) because it was believed that the entire pyramid consisted of such stones. But this is certainly not the case, otherwise you would also see this masonry formation inside. But inside the pyramid looks completely different, like a cave in a mountain. It is therefore clear that the pyramid behind the stones consists of a mountain, a table mountain. This masonry was "leaned" against this mountain, which was formed into a pyramid, because it could not stand on its own as it does not have the appropriate statics.

"The stones of the masonry could" Sahin begins again "indeed had to be stacked evenly and circumferentially on all four sides and, above all, inserted into each other at the corners like a cogwheel in order to achieve the statics and "beauty" of the pyramid".

"So you mean," I continue the sentence, "the builders stood on the internal scaffolding still in place from the fifth step, received the stone that had been raised and laid the masonry stone by stone. In my opinion, all the other theories that scientists have developed here are structural necessities, for example that there was another layer of stone behind this masonry towards the mountain (because a hole in the mountain that was opening up was filled) or that the masonry is slightly recessed inwards (as a result of the "leaning" against the mountain)".

"Anyone can do the test," says Sahin, "if you go onto a scaffold on a building shell - it's enough from the fourth floor upwards - and imagine you're building with bricks. After just a few bricks you have built upwards and without any technical aids you have no orientation as to whether the new bricks are still straight - at an angle. And if this building were a sloping pyramid, it is obvious that there must have been many improvements and improvisations during construction. The infamous "botched construction" still exists today and it occurs when work is carried out by human hands because "man is not perfect".
From a constructional point of view, one should by no means assume today's possibilities.

The pyramid was not yet finished with this masonry, which is particularly visible and dominant today!

Let's look at the drawing again for a better understanding:

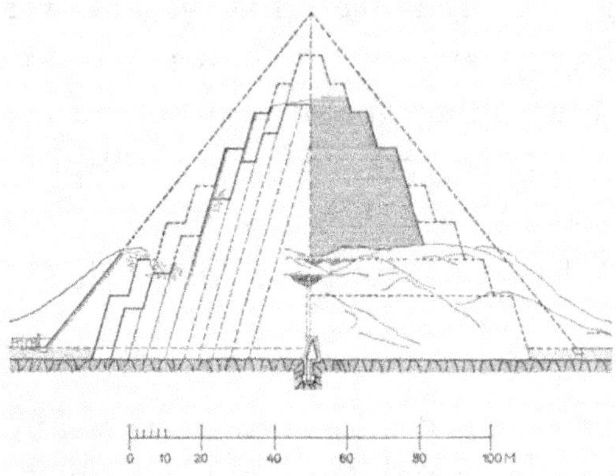

Three-part structure: the core consists of a mesa roughly shaped into a pyramid on which (the stones of the masonry visible today) were piled up and to which in turn a façade (dashed line) was attached. Source 4)

The façade is still missing.

6 **Sixth** step: The façade

The remains of the façade are clearly visible at the top of the Pyramid of Chephren (2015).

For reasons of gravity, the façade can only have been built from the bottom up. An example of this is the pyramid in Meidum, which was built before the pyramid of Cheops.

North side of the pyramid in Meidum Source 4)

The masonry can be seen at the back, on which the façade panels made of sand-lime brick are carefully laid on top of each other. This is probably how the façade of the pyramid of Khufu was constructed. Starting from the ground, the delivered façade stones were stacked on top of each other, stone by stone, leaning against the wall stones and presumably "glued" with gypsum (lime and water components), at least gypsum has a binding effect.

But that's not all.

7 Seventh step: The smoothed façade

In the sixth step, the façade panels were sanded smooth.
This can still be seen clearly on the Mykerionos pyramid. Here, the outer stones were sanded smooth to create the impression of a "smooth façade" (which has since been demolished or stolen, or the work has been stopped again).

The Pyramid of Cheops was also clad with smooth facade stones.
The effect:
When the sun shone on these smooth white façade slabs, it must have had *an impressive radiance*. White in the morning during the day and red-orange-yellow in the evening.
Later, this was also the case with the two other pyramids.

The smoothed stones of the Mykerionos pyramid

Now the location outside the capital Memphis also makes sense because, seen from Memphis, first one of the Cheops pyramids, later three pyramids shining in the sun from late afternoon in the evening sun, shining orange and finally red and thus impressive pyramids could have been seen in the distance! The sun god Rah seemed close enough to touch every day.

Interim conclusion :

The three pyramids in Giza were created in complex steps:

First:

The shaping of each mesa into a pyramid. This was an incredible achievement in view of the mass, both by Hemiun as the genius and by his team and the many other unknown workers.

Secondly:

A masonry of hewn stones was leaned against this mesa, which was *roughly hewn* into a pyramid. This had two major structural advantages: The shape of the building was already predetermined and did not require its own statics, only the working method had to be adapted. In the meantime, the profession of stonemason had probably developed to such an extent that people knew how to work with stone.

Thirdly:

The crowning glory of the building was - as it still is today - the façade, which shone in at least three colors, namely white during the day and orange and red at sunset, and was visible from afar due to its "elevated position". Whouw! one would shout today.

Incidentally, this also answers another question, namely why the successors of Cheops have a smaller pyramid, although it is human nature that successors, especially sons, usually want to outdo their father.

The answer is: they had no choice! They were faced with the decision of either taking the next mesa or not having a pyramid because the failed attempts at Saqqara were certainly a deterrent. The design of a mesa as a pyramid, on the other hand, had already been absolutely successful at Cheops.

However, the next mesa was smaller and stood behind the pyramid of Khufu as seen from the Nile, and the two successors simply had to accept this "disadvantage". Instead, three pyramids shone as one!

However, this could also be the reason why Chephren, the son of Cheops, had the Sphinx carved out of the existing rock as seen from the Nile BEFORE his father, i.e. "in the first row", which - and scientists agree on this - was hewn out of the rock. During the annual flooding of the Nile, it was then largely under water, which in turn explains the caves discovered under the Sphinx. However, the pyramid construction is still not finished.

8 Eighth step: The inner excavation

My companion Achitect Sahin comments:

"As soon as the mesa had the rough shape of the pyramid - probably at the same time - they set about excavating the inside of the mountain. In doing so, they mainly followed the *natural mountain structure*. There was no need for concrete planning at this point, as it was impossible to know what the mountain structure would look like in detail. So you could only work your way forward step by step."

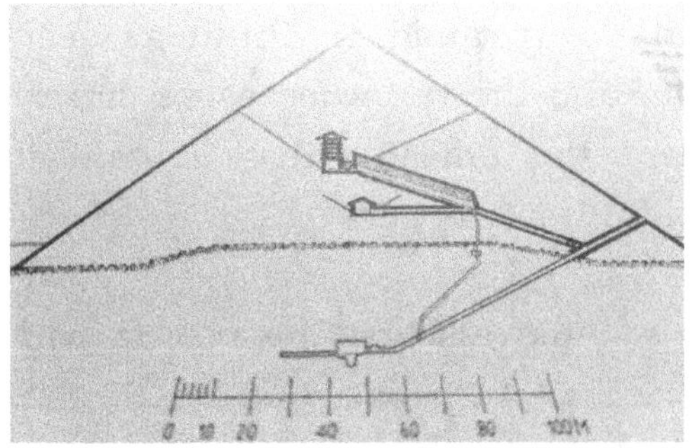

Drawing of the inner structure Source 4)

I once had the opportunity to visit an older disused mine in Germany (Saxony). A small group and I went down into the depths, equipped with flashlights. And surprise: it basically looked similar to the pyramid: a large "gallery" of different stones and mountain structures (minerals) and an up and down "path" with narrow passages. If the mine had been opened for tourists to visit, it would have been refurbished, i.e. simply made a little more "beautiful" and comfortable. This must not have been the case with the pharaoh's tomb back then, but it is obvious.

I just want to say that gorges, narrow passages, high galleries etc. are nothing unusual in mining. Just think of the various beautiful caves that exist around the world.

Entrances as chutes

In the mountain there were most probably natural gorges, holes, caves that were to be made accessible. In order to be able to bring down the resulting enormous stone material, the later entrances in this construction phase - following the force of gravity - probably initially served as chutes for transporting the mountain material *downwards*.

The much smaller people at that time dug tunnels up and down and then let the mining material slide down these tunnels from above. It could then be transported away at ground level.

The interior of the mountain certainly looked very different 4500 years ago than it does today because, as already described at the beginning, many people have "laid hands" here over the millennia and nobody has prevented it. Today we can therefore only make assumptions.

Access today nicely smoothed (for tourists)

9 **Ninth step**: Interior design and completion

Finally, Hemiun probably turned his attention to the actual tomb of the king and queen. Whether the pharaoh's burial chamber was the one that is designated as such today is unlikely, as I have already explained. It could and probably was quite different. In any case, it is likely that Hemiun continued to proceed pragmatically and determined the details of the interior together with the pharaoh and his priests on the basis of the given mountain structure rather than a plan.

An important point was certainly the protected access to the interior of the pyramid, as this was a secret matter to protect against robbers (which, as we know, was in vain). Archaeologists today usually dig down about ten meters to get to the ground level at that time. It is therefore likely that the entrance at that time was also ten meters below ground level, as it cannot be assumed that the priests would have climbed onto a scaffold with the pharaoh's mummy and there was certainly no staircase built, as this would be very visually disturbing. None have been found.

The death cult of the time should also be taken into account. Hemiun himself, for example, is buried in an underground tomb of a mastaba in the western cemetery of the Khufu pyramids (which was also robbed).

16. The burial

It is not known whether the pharaoh Khufu lived to see the completion of the pyramid or whether he was buried in the pyramid at all. As already mentioned, I do not think it likely that he was buried in the sarcophagus that exists today, even if it has no lid.

This granite trough weighing several tons (see next page), finely polished inside and out, could not have been transported upwards on scaffolding and brought to this place in the burial chamber.

Alleged tomb of Cheops Source: Egyptian Museum

In addition, there is a human circumstance against it, because I consider it impossible that priests would have lifted the mummy of the pharaoh on a scaffold and that they themselves would have climbed over this or a new scaffold to perform the ceremonies of the death cult.

If there was a burial of Pharaoh Cheops here, it was also connected with a corresponding ceremony that certainly took place on the ground (and not in the air).

The earlier reports about the different condition are striking. In brief:

 - In 639 AD,

Arabs find in the burial chamber a marble hollow in the center with a lid closed with a lid and rotten bones

- In 1553

Pierre Belon found a chest made of black

marble without a lid and in the the Great Hall (gallery) a fountain with water
- 1580
Jean Palerne and his companion entered the pyramid from above the pyramid and found a deep well in front of a trough without a lid but one piece was broken off
- In 1740
Benoit De Mailett, already mentioned in point 9.3 Benoit De Mailett wrote of a trough with a lid.

The descriptions of the interior of the Pyramid of Cheops are also chaotic.
However, it is possible that ritual acts took place in this room after the pyramid was completed.
Whatever the case, only a few trustworthy people would have known about the actual entrances and the design of the interior of the mountain.
A wall was also built around the pyramid to keep the people at a distance. The trusted people died and the pyramids and pharaohs, six hours' walk away, became a minor matter for the next generations. The pharaohs of the "Old Kingdom" soon became a thing of the past, just as the fame of deceased personalities soon fades.

However, the three kings left behind a striking and lasting "eternal" building.

17. The final result

The Pyramid of Cheops in Giza could not be "built" as a new construction project from the bottom up around 4500 years ago due to a lack of technical equipment.

1 The core structure

First of all, there is *a mesa* inside. It forms the core masonry and thus the *natural statics.*
The core structure was therefore already present as a *natural mountain,* meaning that no statics were needed, no foundations and, above all, the durability was a given due to the mountain structure!

2 Forming the pyramid

This table mountain was shaped into a pyramid *from top to bottom* using scaffolding, hammers, axes, shovels and spades (creadet).

The chipped mountain material could be easily transported away in baskets and wooden sledges by hand or with the help of camels and donkeys. This work was to a certain extent the first construction phase of the "shell", which can be clearly seen elsewhere:

Hierakonpolis c. 2955 - 2635 BC Source 1)

Due to the mountain structure, there were holes and protrusions to the ideal shape so that the roughly hewn mountain still needed an even layer of stones.

3 The masonry

The next step was therefore the masonry that is visible today. Based on the Table Mountain, hewn stones were stacked on top of each other, following the force of gravity from bottom to top. This resulted in a uniform pyramid that was aligned exactly at an angle and was not affected by the weather (especially the wind).

Today, these stones are the striking cladding of the mountain structure behind it, but the façade that completes the building is still missing.

4 The façade

The next step was the façade. It consisted - still partially visible today at the top of the pyramids - of sand-lime bricks that had been ground smooth and could be carried. These sand-lime brick slabs first had to be broken out of the quarry and/or taken directly from the mountain and then shaped into a rectangular form by hand and sanded smooth in the next steps.

In the next, fourth step, the polished slabs had to be carried up to the respective place on the pyramid or pulled up with ropes and transported to the designated place.

The polished slabs were then applied to the masonry on site and presumably fixed with plaster. This plaster was probably the weak point because plaster absorbs moisture and then dissolves, losing its strength and thus the "adhesive function" between the masonry and the façade panels. Result: The façade panels come loose and fall off.

The lower rows could of course simply be stacked and aligned. They have since been used for other purposes.

5 The interior design

Independently of the exterior work, the interior of the mountain could be finished. Entrances and exits were dug and these were also ideal for the removal of the mining material.

The structure of the interior does indeed look as if there was a plan for it. But this was probably not the case. Imagine you are standing in a large unknown cave: you don't know what to do next. If you wanted to dig a passage, you would start where it was possible. In the same way, this complex system is likely to have arisen largely by chance. It is no longer possible to reconstruct it because too many structural changes have been made in the meantime as described.

Unfortunately, we can only see the state as it is *today*. 4500 years ago, the condition could - and probably should - have been different. I personally miss air ducts for the supply of oxygen for the working people and for the torches that were probably invented for the first time (could fire be used now or how else could you work in the dark back then?) or candles as well as for the exhaust air of the dust from the work on the mining material.

The three chambers are also worth a look, especially Kings Chamber No. 10.

British soldiers carried out "thorough destruction work" here in the years around 1800 by blasting with gunpowder. In doing so, they uncovered an inexplicable chamber structure of the Kings Chamber.

It seems clear to me that no man of that time could have built something like this in the middle of a mountain (see below). It must be part of the original structure of Table Mountain.

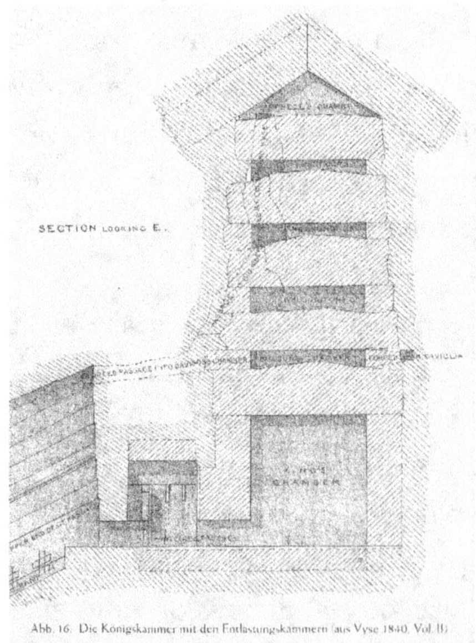

Abb. 16. Die Königskammer mit den Entlastungskammern (aus Vyse 1840, Vol. II)

Chamber structure blown free by British soldiers source 5)

Likewise, if the inside of the mountain was built by human hands, the rising Grand Gallery would also have to have a *static substructure.*

Today, as mentioned, the walls are smooth and braced with iron supports for the safety of tourists. It is therefore no longer possible to determine the original condition.

6 Conclusion

It is therefore probably true that each pyramid consists of three parts, namely
- a rough mountain structure. It ensures the statics
- stacked stones of a sustainable size
  as masonry for the aesthetics of the pyramid
  and at the same time as a support
- of a smoothed façade attached to it
  facade, which is hardly visible today
  as a decorative element of the pyramid.

It has to be said: The construction of the pyramid by Wisir Hemiun for his pharaoh was an ingenious and gigantic masterpiece!

This practical and highly probable solution in no way diminishes the outstanding achievements of Egyptologists to date. They should just realize that the pyramids at that time could *not have been "rebuilt" from the bottom up.*

It is much more likely that they already existed as mesas because they corresponded to the local conditions. There are hundreds of mesas of all sizes along the Nile, which is more than 1000 kilometers long.

In order to have the ultimate certainty, it is not Egyptologists but geologists and mining engineers with today's modern measuring technology who are needed. Only they could check and confirm that each of the pyramids inside is an earlier mesa.

Sources:

ã Pictures without references are from the author

1) Claude Vandersleyen Das Alte Ägypten Propyläen Kunstgeschichte Propyläen Verlag Berlin 1975

2) Kazuyoshi Nomachi/Gerhard Konzelmann Nil Strom der Ströme Verlag Herder Freiburg-Basel-Wien 1989

3) Semsek Hans-Günter Egypt and Sinai Dumont Art Travel Guide DuMont Reiseverlag Ostfildern 2011

4) Müller-Römer Frank The Construction of the Pyramids in Ancient Egypt Herbert Utz Verlag Munich 2011

5) Oeser Erhard Cheops's secret - the scientific conquest of Egypt Verlag Philipp von Zabern Darmstadt/Mainz 2013

6) Von Retyi Andreas Geheimakte Gizeh-Plateau Rätsel unter dem Sand Kopp Verlag Rottenburg 2005 (general information about corridors beneath the Sphinx).

7) Gottschall Christina and Sabine Heilig "Sansibar Reise-Handbuch" Unterwegs Verlag

Manfred Klemann Singen 2001

Websites (general information):

8) Wikipedia Pyramids of Egypt (English)

9) Planet-Wissen.de (German)

10) gizapyramid.com (English)